Zen and Again
The Metaphysical Philosophy of Psychology

Further Ramblings from the internet

Scott Shaw

Buddha Rose Publications

Zen and Again: The Metaphysical Philosophy of
Psychology: Further Ramblings from the Internet
Copyright © 2017 By Scott Shaw All Rights Reserved

Cover Photographs by Scott Shaw
Copyright © 2017 All Rights Reserved

Rear Cover Photograph of Scott Shaw by Hae Won Shin
Copyright © 2017 All Rights Reserved

No portion of this book may be reproduced in any manner without the expressed written permission of the author or the publishing company.

First Edition 2017

ISBN 10: 1-877792-94-2
ISBN 13: 9781877792946

Library of Congress: 2017933735

Printed in the United States of America

10 9 8 7 6 5 4 3 2 1

Zen and Again
The Metaphysical Philosophy of Psychology

Foreword

Here it is, *The Scott Shaw Zen Blog 7.0*, originally presented on the World Wide Web. All of the writings presented in this book were written between October 2016 and February 2017 with a few reaching back to August 2016.

As was the case with the previously published volumes based upon *The Scott Shaw Zen Blog;* entitled: *Scribbles on the Restroom Wall, The Chronicles: Zen Ramblings from the Internet, Words in the Wind, Zen Mind Life Thoughts, The Zen of Life, Lies, and Aberrant Reality, Apostrophe Zen, and The Abstract Arsenal of Zen* this volume is presented exactly as it was viewed on scottshaw.com with no rewriting, punctuation, or typo corrections. From this, we hope you will receive the original reading experience.

This volume of internet ramblings is presented with the date and time listed as to when each blog was originally posted. Also, the blogs in this volume are presented from last to first. With this, we hope to present a transcendence back through time as opposed to an evolving evolution. In addition, we left out the traditional *Table of Contents* in an attempt to leave this volume with a much more free-flowing reading experience.

As a note: the aphorisms that were written during this period of time are present in the second section of this book beginning on page 203.

Okay, there's the information and the definitions. Read on… We hope you enjoy it. And, be sure to stayed tuned for the ongoing *Scott Shaw Zen Blog* @ scottshaw.com.

How Can You Help?
Who Should You Help? Why Should You Help?
03/Feb/2017 08:54 AM

Do you spend any time thinking about how you can help another person? If you don't, this says a lot about you.

Do you spend any time thinking about how you can make someone else's life better? If you don't, this says a lot about you.

Do you ever go out of your way to help someone, give someone something? Do you ever do this for someone that you want nothing from in return? If you don't this says a lot about you.

When you need help—when you are feeling bad, unhappy, depressed, need a loan, who do you turn to? When you turn to that person or persons are they there for you? Do they give you the help that you need? If they do, how does that make you feel? If they don't, how does that make you feel?

Have you ever needed help and there was no one there to help you? What impact did that have on your life and how did you recuperate?

Many people spend no time at all thinking about the feelings and the needs of anyone else but themselves and/or those they love. At best, someone may give a dollar to a bum or put some money in the collection plate at church. But, is this truly helping anyone? Does it actually change one person's life for the better—that one person who really needs your help? You may feel better about yourself for doing it, but does it truly help anyone? Does it truly change anyone's life for the better?

If you don't think about other people, if you don't care about other people, if you experience the emotion of pride or happiness when you witness other people being hurt or suffering, what does that say about you?

It is easy to be cavalier in life. It is easy to be bold and demeaning of others when you are in a position of completeness. But, what happens when you are not? No one is whole, complete, and unhurt forever. Everyone eventually needs help. What happens when you need help but you have built your life upon helping no one?

Think about your moment right now. What are you planning to do with your day? Do your plans only involve you: what you want, what you desire, what will make you feel good? Do you have any intention of helping anyone else?

Most people never think about other people in terms of reaching out a helping hand. They think about themselves. They plan how they can get over on a person they may not like. They think what do, *"I,"* want and how can, *"I,"* make my today better for, *"Me."*

What are you thinking about? Are you thinking about yourself? Or, are you planning how you can actually go out, do something positive, and help someone?

In life, it is easy to take. In life, it is easy to judge. In life, it is easy to think only about yourself. But, what kind of life will you have lived if you do not think and care about other people?

Ask yourself, *"Who can I help today?"* Now, ask yourself, *"Are you willing to help them?"* Are you willing to care enough about someone else that you actually go out of your way, stop thinking only about yourself, and do something for them—do something good that actually helps them?

We all need help. We all need kindness. We all need love. Are you willing to give it? If not, what does that say about you?

The Perception of Reality
02/Feb/2017 07:44 AM

Is it better to have fourteen one dollar bills or one one-hundred-dollar bill? The bills are all made out of the same paper. They all look pretty much the same. And, more is always better; isn't it?

Is it better to live in a very large house with a lot of rooms or a small apartment? Bigger is always better; right? More is always more; right?

Is it better to have a job that pays you a lot money or to have a lot of free time? With money you can buy yourself all kinds of new things; right? And, without a job how will you get the money you need to buy yourself the things you desire?

Life is defined by your perception of reality. Life is defined by what you were taught and how you were taught to encounter it. What you were taught to want is defined by what you were told is important.

If you did not know what number was on a dollar bill more would be better; wouldn't it? But, as you do, as detailed in the previous word problem, more is less. But, is it? What is paper money but a concept that we are taught to believe in. Does that piece of paper actually have any true value if we all did not agree that it does?

If you are in the wilderness and there is no one else around, what value would that piece of paper have? Yet, people spend their entire life chasing it. How about you?

Most people desire to live in a large grand house. They want to own it. But, how can you own it? You must have the money to buy it. How and where do you get that money? Some people are given it buy their family. That's nice but most of us are not so lucky. Thus, most must spend all of their time doing something that they do not want to do; i.e. their job, simply so they can afford to live in that house. Once the down payment is saved up and made on the house, the monthly mortgage payments must be paid and, if anything goes wrong with the house, one has to come up with the money to pay for those repairs. Buying a house takes most people away from living life as all of their life and financial focus must be place on that house.

This leads us to the job. We all need a way to pay for the way we live. But, the more things that you must have to live your life in the manner you have decided to live it, the more those things cost, thus, the more money you must generate. Money… You know that paper thing that has no true value.

A job takes most of the time from a person's life away. They must go to a place at a certain time each day and do what they are required to do to get paid for being there. Yes, it is a necessary way to survive but it takes the everything away from the lives of most people. At the end of their days are they are left with was a life defined by nothing more than what they did to pay for the house they desired to live in.

Do you ever study the elements that come to define your life? Do you ever think about how what you desire will cost you and your life? Do you ever think about the reality of reality and question how you are the primary player in accepting its suchness and, as such, you are the causation factor for your all and your everything?

You believed it. You chose it. You did what it took to get it and now what? What will your life actually add up to based upon the desires you have desired and what it took to get them?

Interpreting Someone Else's Reality
31/Jan/2017 09:08 AM

Have you ever heard someone talking on the phone and they were making some kind of statement about something and you thought that you knew what they were talking about? You thought you had them totally figured out. But, did you? You were only hearing one side of the conversation. You have no idea what was being said on the other end of the line, nor do you have any true understanding about what is going on in the mind of the person whom you heard speaking.

Have you ever been talking to someone, perhaps on the phone, and you notice that someone is listening to you. First of all, that is not a nice thing to do. It is none of their business. But, unconscious, unthinking, people do it all the time. They want distraction from their life-boredom so they seek that distraction wherever it may be found.

But, more to the point… Have you ever been talking on the telephone and you realize if someone heard what you just said they would totally not get any of the backstory to what was actually going on and what caused you to say what you said?

This is the thing, people interpret other people's reality by what they have experienced, by what they are experiencing, and by their own self-defined interpretation of reality. From this, they cast judgment onto the conversations of others. Most people are not whole enough onto themselves to simply ignore what they hear. Instead, they wish to interpret it. They wish to judge it. They wish to compare their life to someone else's life—the life that they are hearing being spoken about.

Have you ever seen or heard people you do not know argue? I think most of us have and it is uncomfortable. When this situation occurs, some people stop and stare. They want to see what is going on. They want to become part of the melodrama. They want to compare their life to the words that are being spoken, defining the life of someone else. But, they are not that person or persons. Even if two people are both expressing the reason for their dissatisfied with the other person, anyone who listens does not and cannot understand the internal reality of that couple's relationship and/or what is motivating them both to be guided towards verbal confrontation.

When you are conversing with someone and a stranger is listening, you may be able to explain to that stranger why you are saying what you are saying. Though you may be able to explain why you are saying what you are saying and why you are feeling what you are feeling, no-one is you. And, the truth be told, no one can truly understand you no matter how much of an explanation you provide. At best, all anyone can do is to interpret your reality based upon what they already believe and what they have previously experienced.

Thus, if someone is talking, never listen to them because, not only is it an invasion of another person's privacy, but you can and will never understand what is truly going on in that other person's mind. You are you. They are they. Everyone is outside of everyone else. And, no one can truly ever understand anyone else.

Raising a Ruckus
31/Jan/2017 07:55 AM

For some reason some people like to go out there into the world and raise a ruckus. They like to take their own brand of personal anger and broadcast it to the world. Why do they do this? Because they are not in touch enough with their own emotions to define why they are feeling what they are feeling and to realize that anger is the lowest level of all human emotions and it is simply created by an undefined dissatisfaction within themselves.

The problem is, you can tell them this but they will more than likely deny it. They will have justification(s) for behaving the way they are behaving.

Some people internalize their anger. I know this one young girl who signs her posts, *"I'm screaming on the inside."* Obviously her anger in internalized but she knows that it is there, acknowledges that it exists but, like many people, does not know how to rid herself of it—she doesn't have the cure for the disease. I feel for her.

There are other people who spread their anger out to the internet. It is easy to spread anger there as people are faceless and nameless. But, out there in cyberspace all you find are other faceless, nameless people and whatever you do is ultimately meaningless as it is an action of no-action. An action of no-action not like Zen but an action of no-action based in the fact that it only adds to the hurt, dissatisfaction, and damnation of the world. Thus, and as-such, the harm that it instigates is only reinternalized into the individual who is feeling and express it as there is no one out there who actually cares about the individual unleashing their anger and, thus, there is no one who can help.

Some people want to broadcast their anger. Since the dawning of the video and then the digital age I have watched as some people, defined by their anger, go out into the world with their camera in hand and film themselves being antisocial and angry in public places. Then, they put it up on some website. To them, they are being revolutionary. To the rest of the world they are forced to encounter another person's life dissatisfaction—something no one else wants anything to do with it. Yet, they are forced to encounter it. This is never a good thing—bringing other people into your anger filled actions. It only creates negative karma for the instigator.

I think back to the early days of punk rock. There were those of us who felt that we were part of a revolution. But, due to the nature of the beast, it was a violent revolution. Within this genre, some people found a vehicle in which to unleash their internal anger outwards onto others. In the early days, all was fine. Then, slam dancing became a place for those who were not truly a part of the scene to unleash their physical violence. I would watch as Marines from Camp Pendleton would come up to Hollywood and jump into the pit simply to start a fight. Why? Why would a trained fighter need to do this? Simply to show that they were a trained fighter? No, if someone is truly trained and content within themselves they never need to behave in this manner. It was simply a means for these people to unleash their dissatisfaction outwards onto others.

I also think back to a well-known proponent of Bruce Lee's *Jeet Kune Do* who trained *Seal Team Six* in self-defense applications. He spoke how his trainees and himself would go out to bars, start fights, to test themselves. Finally, in his forties, he decided he had to stop doing that. But, why does anyone, by whatever self justification, need to spread their own dissatisfaction with the world outwards from themselves? Simply to test their skills? That is a poor excuse for inducing injury to other people. All this type of behavior does is to damage the lives of other people. And, that is never a good thing.

Sure, all of these people have a reason for doing what they do. A reason emanating from within their own mind.

But, it is their mind. It is not my mind; it is not your mind. They are taking the misplaced emotions that are reverberating within themselves and broadcasting it outwards to the world. Thus, they spread their negativity and their dissatisfaction that is solely emanating from with themselves and their life onto others. From this, all kinds of realms of negative karma is born. This is why, when you look at a person doing this now and see them again in ten years, twenty years, or thirty years, nothing has changed with their life, they are still dominated by their undefined, misplaced, unrecognized anger which leads to them lashing out at the world.

If you are angry, and many people are, it is what you choose to do with that anger that defines what kind of person you truly are.

Who are you? As you so out of control of yourself that you feel you have the right to broadcast your anger and life-dissatisfaction outwards to the world? If you do, you should really look at your life, who you are, why you are, and why you are not whole-enough to take control of your emotions instead of letting them be in control of you.

You make this world. You set your own course of destiny into motion. This course of destiny is defined by what you choose to do with your life and how you choose to react to the emotions that are only felt by you.

The Small Things
27/Jan/2017 08:34 AM

Though people forever have their eyes on the big things that they want, it is the small things that comes to define all of our lives.

"We are all in the gutter, but some of us are looking at the stars," to quote Oscar Wilde. We all want to be grand, live grand, and do grand things. We all want to be on top of the game. This being the case, it is actually the small things that come to define our life. ...The small things that we do and/or, in many cases, the small things that we never even consciously think about doing—we just do them; those things come to be the definition of our existence.

Moreover, though everybody wants to be grand, do grand things, very few people ever take the steps to achieve that grandness. They may think about doing something, they may talk about doing this or that, they may discuss those who have achieved what they hope to achieve, but the small thing of talking is all that many have to show for their entire life.

What are you doing today? Maybe you are going to work—a small thing that defines the life of many people. Maybe you are taking care of your kids—a small, necessary thing, that comes to define the lives of many people. Maybe you are going to school—a small thing that many people do with the belief that schooling will make them something more—something other than something small.

Small things are necessary for survival. But, are you unconsciously dominated by them or are you consciously aware of their implications?

It is also the small things that can come to define the life of a person unintentionally. You fall down, break you arm. Your life, at least for a time, comes to be defined by that small accidental action. I have known people that we doing construction work or factory work and have cut themselves very badly; damaging their body. This small action, changed the rest of their life. They did not intend for this small thing to come to define their life but it did. I knew a person who was working on a car and the other mechanic turned it on and chopped off all his fingers that were in the engine fan—a small thing; turning on the car, and the rest of his life completely altered. Yesterday, I saw a young man in his souped-up Mustang burning rubber and then speeding up a residential street that generally has a lot of children on it. What if he would have hit one of those children—which has happened to many people through out the evolution of car society. His life, the child's life would have been changed forever. This, all by doing a small, foolish, youthfully motivated thing. Small can equal big.

Every thought you think, every word you speak, every action you take defines what your life will ultimately become. Small or large, those things will come to define what you have have done and what you will next be able to do with your life.

All of our lives are dominate by the small things that we do. Start studying the small things of your life for they will ultimately define who and what you are.

There is Always an Excuse Why Not to Help
25/Jan/2017 08:54 AM

How often do you go out of your way to help someone? How often do you do something nice for someone simply because you can?

There is always a reason for you to do something nice for yourself. …Then you get what you want. …Then one of your desires will be fulfilled. …Then you will feel better. But, how often do you step outside of yourself—step outside of the getting what you want and actually do something to make someone else's something somewhat better?

Most people spend their entire life thinking solely about themselves. Maybe the people that they love are added into this equation. But, that love is also based upon thinking about themselves. The person they love gives them something that they want—this answers a need that they have. Thus, love is a very selfish emotion.

People do things all the time to make themselves feel better, more empowered, more whole, more something… People cast judgments all the time to make themselves feel like they are the knower—they want the world to believe that they are the knower. But, people generally never study why they are feeling what they are felling nor why they are doing what they are doing. They simply do. They simply do to make themselves feel better. From this, people only do for themselves. This is a very selfish and uncaring mindset.

What about the people out there? What about the other people? Do you ever think or care about what they are feeling? Do you ever think or care about what they are experiencing? Do you ever think about how what you are doing is affecting their life? If you don't, what does that say about you?

If is very easy to do something for someone you like. It is very hard to do something for someone you don't like. But, do you ever take the time to study why you like a specific person? Do you ever take the time to study why you don't like a specific person?

If you take the time to understand why you are feeling something about someone you will more than likely come to the conclusion that what you are feeling is based upon your own preconceived notions about that person and not necessarily upon facts. But, moreover, remove your projection of what you believe another person to be from this formula and then what do you have? You have a person who is no longer defined by what you think about them—no more, no less; just a human being.

Doing positive things for people is a good thing. Saying positive things about people is a good thing. Helping people, when you see that they need help, is a great thing.

Some people falsely believe that helping is only defined by donating large sums of money, going and feeding homeless people at a homeless shelter, or helping the lepers in India. Sure, this helping… But, helping is also defined by doing small things. …Correcting small evils when you see or hear them. Picking something up when someone has dropped it. Or, simply choosing to leave any space you enter a bit better because you were there.

Really… Certainly don't do bad, judgmental, self-serving, or negativity things. But, more than that, stop making excuses for helping. Wherever you are, do something good that make the overall-all better. Help!

One Minute Later
25/Jan/2017 08:19 AM

Have you ever been in a car or a motorcycle accident? How did that accident affect your life? For most, these events are a negative experience—negative, especially if you were hurt or your car or motorcycle was badly damaged.

Now, think about this… What if you had left home one minute later that day. One minute later or one minute earlier and you would not have been at that intersection, at that point in time, where that accident took place. Thus, you would have never been in that accident.

This goes to show you how your life is dominated by simple movements—movements that can change your everything. A choice to leave, when you choose to leave, and everything in your life is changed forever.

I have been in a few serious accidents in my life. Going back to my childhood, when I was maybe two or three, (I remember very far back in my life), a car hit my father late at night. This was my first accident experience. My father, at the time, own a restaurant near the USC campus and we were driving home at maybe one or two AM; whenever the restaurant closed. I was sitting on my mother's lap. This was long before child car seats or even seat belts. The car hit us. I apparently smacked my head on the dash due to the impact. Though I don't remember that part. My father, obviously pissed off due to this fact, gets out and the black guy that hit us pulls a knife on my father. …Things were sketchy back then too. My father, a petty savvy fighter, knocked him out. The cops soon showed up and the guy was arrested.

But, think about it… Had we left the restaurant just a few minutes sooner or a few minutes later, none of that melodrama would have happened.

When I was ten, I was driving in a car near Valentine, Arizona with my uncle. It was the winter. We were driving on Route 66. I so clearly remember as this pickup truck drives up next to us, looks at us, and passes us very quickly. I took notice as the two people in the truck were long haired Native Americans. As this was 1968 you took notice of a man's hair length. Instead of just passing us, however, they intentionally cut us off, causing my uncle to react and, due to the fact the road was icy, we swerved off the road and flipped the car. Why they did this, I don't know. Drunk? Maybe. Because we had California license plates? Maybe. Or, just to fuck with us. I don't know... But, it was quite an experience. One that should never have happened. It was the first time that I believed I was going to die—in one of those seconds that seems to last for an eternity. I let go of life. But, I lived and I was okay. Okay, but never the same.

I have been hit while driving my motorcycle a few times. Two of those times were very serious. My life was never the same... Hell, my friend even ran into me with his motorcycle as we were driving down the Sunset Strip back in the late 70s. He was trying to pick up on these two girls in a car and wasn't paying attention. He hit my bike, we both hit the payment. The girls laughed and drove off. Life...

I've been in a few smaller accidents, as well, but the one thing that any one who has even been in an accident, large or small, will tell you is that they are not fun. They are an occurrence that comes out of the blue—an occurrence that you wish never happened. An occurrence that can truly change your life.

But, any of those accidents—they did not have to happen. All I had to do was leave a minute earlier or a moment later. But, I did not. Why not?

Accidents also go to the situations when you meet a new person by chance. You are there, they are there and, for whatever reason, you begin a conversation. This conversation may equal great things in your life. It may also equal devastation. A chance meeting, by accident, yet your life is altered forever. Had you not been there, had they not been there, none of the anything would have ever happened. But, you were there, they were there, and now your life has come to be defined by this interaction. An accidental meeting, yet it comes to define you.

Some would say that all things that happen to you are god's will. Others would call up the karma card. Still others will say it was destiny. Maybe... It could be anyone one of those things if you choose to be a believer. But, life is random. Life happens. Different things, different experiences, happen to all of us. From them, we become who we are.

Some people want to find a reason for no reason. Some people wish to attribute logic and a causation factor to everything so that they may feel like there is something bigger going on—that god has a purpose for them. But, this is all mental masturbation. It is simply people looking for a reason why when there is no reason why.

Life happens. You are here. You do things. You make choices when to do things. From this, your life becomes defined by the experiences you have when you are doing the things you choose to do when you choose to do them.

Reason, logic, justification, they are only there if you believe they are there. But, what does the other person who was part of the accident believe? Probably something totally different from what you are believing. Thus, there is no fact—only supposition.

Life... Though we all wish we could find a reason why, there is no reason why.

You've Done Some Bad Bad Things
24/Jan/2017 09:46 AM

Have you ever had something negative happen to you and you think back to a time when you did something to someone and think, *"There it is. I'm getting paid back for my karma."* You experience the event, you think that thought, you believe your karmic debt is paid up, but your life does not get any better. Why is that? Because it is not you (or anyone else for that matter) who can truly understand the complexities of karma and life debt.

The reason I discuss karma quite frequently is because people are always referring to it. It has nothing to do with religion, philosophy, or anything like that... It is just that it has become such a common belief in modern society that everyone references it. People talk about it all the time. But, what no one understands is that no one is so wise to truly understand the subtleties of karma.

All karma begins with you. If you say something bad, if you are judgmental or hurtful, if you do something bad, then you should receive your karma for that action, right? But, what is the appropriate karma? If you hurt anyone, through either conscious or unconscious action, you should get your karmic payback, yes? But, no one wants to get paid back for what they have done that has hurt someone or something else. At best, they justify their actions. Perhaps, they believed they were right in what they said or did. They believe they had the right. They don't care about the injury they unleashed. But, the fact is, no one has the right to hurt anyone or anything for any reason, whether consciously or unconsciously. Thus, here is the birthplace of karma.

Ask yourself, is there someone out there who believes that you hurt their life? If they believe that you hurt their life, then you did hurt their life.

Now, ask yourself, do you believe you had the right to hurt their life? If your answer is, *"Yes,"* first of all, that is a very selfish, unthinking, and uncaring answer. And, if your answer is, *"Yes,"* now turn the tables on yourself. Is there someone out there who has hurt you? Do you believe they had the right to unleash that injury? Probably not.

You see, this is where the entire concept and ideology of karma becomes so complex. There are some people, in fact many people out there, who do not even think or care about anyone else but themselves. If you express to them that they hurt you or damaged your life, they don't care. They may make excuses, give you justifications, or turn the blame around on you. As unconscious, uncaring, and unthinking as that is, that is the mind frame from where many people operate. Looking from the outside we can all say, *"That is not right."* But now, look at yourself. Have you ever behaved in that manner? Have you ever hurt someone and not cared? Have you ever hurt someone by saying something or doing something that injured the life of that person? Did you do this either because you were not conscious enough to realize what your action may instigate or perhaps you believed you had the right? But, did you? Do you have the right to hurt anyone for any reason? Do they have the right to hurt you?

If you think you have the right to hurt anyone for any reason, you are wrong. If you think you have the right to judge anyone for any reason, and your judgments hurts someone, you are wrong. If your actions, whether conscious or unconscious, intentional or unintentional, hurts anyone or anything for any reason, you are wrong. From this wrong, negative karmic pay back will come your way.

Okay… Now, that this is established, think about this, *"What would be the appropriate karmic payback for what you did to that person that believes you hurt their life?"* Take a moment right now. Think about the people that you hurt. Think about the people that believe that you hurt them. Think about how you hurt them. What will pay them back for what you did to them? What has to happen to your life to make them feel better about what you did?

This is the thing… Each action that you do sets forth an entire course of events that no one can anticipate or predict. What you say, who you say it to, what you do, who you do it to, creates an entire universe onto itself. For this reason, the conscious person becomes very thoughtful about what they say and what they do. They wish to hurt no one. They intentionally hurt no one. They put their ego in check and they control themselves. They wish to set no negative events into motion. But, the unconscious, the self righteous, the empowered, and the self involved person doesn't think about anything or anyone but themselves. They believe they have the right to say or do anything that they wish. From this, a plethora of unknown, un-chartable events are set into motion in their life which ultimately equals a lot of bad karma coming their direction.

If you live your life based upon negativity and hurt, doing damage to the life of other people—if you justify your actions, believing that you have the right to take, say, or do anything that you wish; what do you believe will be the repercussions to your life? What will be your karma? What will you have to go through to pay back those you have injured? The fact is, no one knows and no one can predict the answer to that question.

Therefore, the next time you encounter a bad experience and think your karma is paid up, think again.

How Do You Want to Be Remembered?
23/Jan/2017 08:40 AM

As people pass through life many begin to think about how they will be remembered once they are gone.

…Let me paraphrase here… Many people, (perhaps even most), think about nothing. They just do what they do until they can do it no longer. Motivated by desire, greed, lust, anger, and selfishness they pass through their existence while never thinking about the big picture of who they are, what they are, how other people see them, and how they will be remembered. Many do this until they are very close to the doors of death and then they may wonder. But, then it is too late.

Some people also find ways to maintain an abstracted mindset. Drugs, (whatever that drug may be), is one of the big ones. In an altered state people find all kinds of misaligned facts and ideologies to justify what they are thinking, what they are doing, and why. But, as has long been studied, people who partake of these intoxicants, for an extended period of time, damage their cognitive skills to the degree that they began to constantly seek new reasons and justifications to enter that altered state. They want to get high. They want to get drunk. They want to get whatever… But, by whatever name and/or whatever ideological justification one may concoct, *"High,"* is not reality. It is not the way we, as human beings, were meant to experience life. Thus, all thoughts and ideas born from this reality are false truths.

Is high the way you want to be remembered? Meaning, you were not whole enough onto yourself to encounter a real life. Is that who you are?

Okay, with that of the way, let's get to the primary subject of this discussion, how do you want to be remembered?

Take a look at your life right now—look at the things you have done and said up until this point in time. With those things defined, how would you be remembered if you left this life place right now? Is that the way you would like to be remembered?

Take a look at what you have put out there about yourself; the things that you have said or done. When other people look at them how will they define who you are?

People rarely think about the fact that what they say about themselves, the way they describe themselves to the world is one of the key factors to how the rest of the world perceives them and, thus, how they will be remembered.

With this as a basis, right now, take a look at what you have said, what you have done, and what you have put out there to the world about yourself. Is that how you would like to be a remembered, as a…? With what is out there about you; what you have said and done, what others have said, is that how you would like to be remembered?

This brings us to an important point in this discussion, *"Other people."* People say things about other people all the time. Some of them are nice, revering, and uplifting; others are negative. In either case, what other people say about a person may be based in truths, half truths, or flat out lies. Though this is where the definition of, *"You,"* may become dicey, it is not the thing that should define your life.

People say what they say about other people based upon any number of self-motivated ideologies. As in all cases, good is always good and equals good. Bad, on the other hand, is always bad and equals negativity. The person who says and does good things encounters positivity in their life. The person who says and does negative things will continually find their life being bombarded by negativity. That is just the way it is.

This being said, your life is defined by what YOU actually say and do. No matter what someone else says about you, if it is not true, if it is not based in the truth of who you truly are, all those false and negative words will ever come to do is ultimately define the life of the other person, as they are the one saying them. Remember any negative word spoken about anyone else only come back to define the life of the person who spoke them and not the person they are speaking about. Any word spoken in anger, frustration, or jealousy only turns around on the person who uttered it as they are the one instigating the negativity. Therefore, if you embrace the positive in all aspects of your life, that will be the ultimate outcome of how you will be defined. There is the high road and there is the low road. Which one are you walking upon?

People interact in life all the time. Some of these interactions turn out to be positive but many also turn out to be negative. That is just life. But, it is what you do with those negative experiences that will ultimately define you as a person. Sure, you may be angered by a negative experience you have with a person or a situation but it is how you cope and deal with that anger that will define your life.

When you are angry with someone or something, how do you deal with it? Do you study it and learn from the experience? Or, do you just lash out and spread your anger and negativity, that was motivated by the situation, out to the world? Maybe you think those words and those actions will make you feel better. And, maybe they do for a moment. But, what they also do is to add to the definition of your life.

…How other people see you. …How you will be remembered. And, this takes us back to the point of this discourse; what you do, what you say, how you do what you do, defines how you will be remembered. You are the one putting it all out there. You are the one deciding to act in a specific manner. You are the one casting the mold for your life. If you are embracing the negative, if you are broadcasting the negative, if you are reinvigorating the negative, the negative will hunt you down, as you are the one who invoked and re-invoked it and that will come to be the definition of your life.

Right now, look at your life… Are you where you want to be? Are you doing what you want to be doing? Do other people see you the way you want to be seen? And, how responsible are you for any of it? Many people shift the blame. Many people forever blame someone or something else. Do you?

Where you are in life, who you are in life, has been defined by what you have done, what you have said, how you have acted and reacted to all of the events that we each go through in life. Thus, there is no one to blame for anything but yourself—you made the choice to do what you made the choice to do. Thus, there is only you to blame. As long as you attempt to shift the blame to others, as long as you continually choose to talk about others in any sense of the negative, all that comes to do is define your life as the person who does not take responsibility for their own choices and actions. Is that how you want to be remembered?

Be the best person you can be. Don't say or do negative things. Do take things from other people. Don't believe you have the right to judge anyone. Be more than any negativity that you encounter in your life and you will be remembered well.

How do you want to be remembered? Remember, that definition begins and ends with what you choose to do.

Discussing What You Don't Really Know
20/Jan/2017 04:45 PM

Do you ever find yourself discussing a person you have never met? Do you ever find yourself talking about a subject that you have never really studied? Do you ever find yourself speaking about something that you have never really done? Do you ever speak as an expert, making other people believe that you know the truth, when you have no inside knowledge only speculation?

If you weren't there then you weren't there. If you don't know the person you don't know the person. If you have never played the game you don't understand what it takes to play the game.

Why do you discuss anyone else at all? What do you speak about abstract subjects at all? Why do you believe you have the answers on a subject you have never lived? Why do you think you can play the game better than the people who actually play the game?

Life is a complete intermixing of mind stuff and life stuff. People think. Because they think they want to know. Because people want answers about what they are thinking about some people present themselves as someone who has the answers to what other people are questioning.

People speak of god and holy figures because there is no way to prove them wrong. These holy entities are either so all-encompassing or so-dead that there is no way to question what a person who claims to be presenting the truth about them is saying. But, people are alive. Why do you, why does anyone, talk about them as if they know anything? How many people have you heard speaking as if they are experts on a specific person but, in truth, they are totally wrong? How can anyone present themselves as an expert on any person? Especially, if the person is still alive. As such, again, we go back to one of the primary questions, why are you spending your time discussing another person when whatever it is you are saying will more than likely be incorrect?

People speak on subjects that they have never experienced. These subjects are as many as the mind can conceive but why do they speak about them if they have not and will not ever personally experience them?

In life, if you are not doing, you are not doing. Talking is not doing. Talking is only talking. What does talking equal? It only equals talking. It does not equal anything that is real.

Some people present themselves as experts. But, how can they be an expert if they are not the person they are speaking about, have not done what the person they are speaking about has done, and is not actively training their body and their mind to be anything but a person who is calming to be an authority on someone or something else when they have accomplished nothing with their own life?

You really need to think about what you are doing with your life. You really need to look at how you spend your time. You really need to look at whom you are listening to. For all knowledge is based upon only one things; experience. It is not based on conversation. Why waste you life-time ideally talking.

I Want My Umbrella!
20/Jan/2017 03:51 PM

The drought has finally broken in So. Cal. and it is raining like crazy this year. I was never too worried about it. Way back when I was taking a climatology class, as I was working towards my B.A. in Geography, I learned that weather goes through cycles—for a time it will be very stable and predictable and then it will go into an erratic period. In any case, it is now raining a lot...

I was going into a store today. A lady and her young daughter, maybe three years old, had gotten out of their car and they were walking under the cement awning. They were not getting wet but the little girl wanted her umbrella. The mother kept saying she didn't need it but the little girl wanted it. She began screaming in baby talk, *"I want my umbrella!"* They entered the store and the screaming continued. It just went on and on and on... I could not help but think to the way people are raising their kids today, compared to how I was raised. If I would have behaved like that I would have been slapped very hard in the face or spanked right there. I learned very young how one must behave.

But, kids aren't like that any more. They are raised totally differently. I watch how some of my extended family members raises their children—they let them get away with anything. They just talk to them but never discipline them.

I believe that for the most part this is based in the violent way my generation was raised. They don't want their kids to go through that. And, I get it. I mean, you look to all the news about how celebrities are being investigated just for spanking their kids. That's crazy. I mean, even when I was in junior high school you could see that the assistant principal emanated so much misguided sadomasochistic, sadistic happiness when he got to pull out the long paddle and hit the students with it when we did something that he deemed wrong. All of the people who did that are probably dead by now but can you imagine if some assistant principal did that in today's world? He'd be in jail. But, the doing of that took place just a couple of decades ago.

Now, I've personally never had any kids. That was a very conscious decision on my part. ...Let the abhorrent bloodline end with me. As such, I certainly understand that I have no right to tell any parent how to raise their kids and I do not. Furthermore, I totally get why some parents let their children run wild. But, I also question what is going to happen to these kids when they become adults and they have to enter the real-world. What are they going to do when they cannot say anything they want, do anything they want, and/or behave in any way they want? I don't know? I think we may be breeding a world of people who are not going to know how to actually survive and interact in the real world.

Getting to Where You Don't Want to Be
20/Jan/2017 07:57 AM

For each of us we have something that we really want to do with our life and we each have things that we really dislike. The problem is, in many cases, to get to doing what we really want to do we have to do something that we don't like.

Then, there is other side of the issue; working and working to get where you want to be and never arriving... All this goes, part-and-parcel, to the process of life.

For me, I hate being in traffic jams. They just seem like such a waste of time. I mean, you know where you started, you know where you want to be, you know how long it should take you to get there but then, in the from-here-to-there, is all that traffic. Living in L.A. comes hand-in-hand with this as you have to drive everywhere. There is no good subway system like in Tokyo, Hong Kong, London, or New York. Though they are trying to develop one, it won't happen in my lifetime. So, all I have ever known is driving and, thus, driving in traffic jams. I hate it.

Anyway, I was sitting on the freeway in a rainy traffic jam yesterday en route to the NAMM show. For those of you who may not know the NAMM show is held at the Anaheim Convention Center once a year and all of the musical instrument manufactures from across the globe come to show their wares. For a musician it is heaven—it is great as you get seey, touchy, feely all that is new.

The thing about the NAMM show is that it is not easy to get into. You either have to be a member, (which has tons of requirement), be an instrument creator, or be an invited guest. Meaning, it is not like *Comic Con* where you can just go and buy a ticket. It is not easy to get in.

This being said, there are thousands and thousands of people who attend each year, coming from all over the world. As my lady likes to title them, *"A bunch of old, ugly, white guys, with long hair."* I guess that makes me one. ☺

Anyway, as I was walking around yesterday, viewing all the stuff, I realized that all of the people who were there were musicians or they would not be there. They all could play their instrument, whatever that instrument may be. And, I am sure many of them were very-very good with their instrument. Sure, sprinkled in among the masses is the occasional rock or pop star, but for most of these people no one has ever seen their face and no one knows their name.

The thing about musicians is, and I realized this decades ago, some of the best musicians I have ever known never became famous. They were great musicians, they desired musical fame, but they never made it. And, unlike people who come to Hollywood with hopes of movie stardom, based solely upon their personal belief that they are pretty, talented, or that they deserve it, (maybe they even take some acting classes), but they are not like musicians who constantly practice and play their instruments, becoming, in many cases, virtuosos in their own right. Virtuosos that the world never hears. They may play in bars, night clubs, hotel lounges, street corners, or in their living room, but the greater world out-there will never knows who they are. Yet, here they are at the NAMM show. All wondering around, living their life, doing what they must do to survive, getting old, while they play their instrument.

Certainly, there is a metaphysical element to all of this in that one could say that playing music is the perfect meditation onto itself and simply by playing, wherever it is you are playing, you are giving back to the overall goodness of the world. But, though all true musicians will attest to the fact that playing their instrument becomes a deep meditation, for most, that is not why they do it. They want to be heard. Thus, they spend their entire life, attempting to get from here to there. …Trying to be heard and seen. Are they enjoying the pathway? I guess each one would have a different answer. But, the one common factor is that they are trying to move from here to there. ...Be something more and bigger.

Life is a pathway. We are here, yet we want to be there. How many people are totally whole, content, and living in a space with no desire? Few, I would guess. But, that does not mean that we cannot learn to accept the pathway; learn to accept and love our time in a traffic jam. Awh, never mind... Life is just the process from here to there. We live, we desire, we want to be something and somewhere else, then we die. We can try to pretend that the pathway is enough, that we are happy in accepting who, where, and what we are but, the fact is, most of us are not happy and content. We want more. A more, that most of us will never know. Welcome to reality.

Own Your Anger
19/Jan/2017 07:18 AM

Many people spend their entire life defined by unhappiness, dissatisfaction, and anger. The reason their life is defined by these very negative emotions is that they do not take the steps to correct this pattern and from this lack of self-directed discipline spend their entire lifetime emoting the remnants of these emotions out to the world.

The internet is the hotbed for people to spew their anger outwards. In times gone past, one of the primary locations for anger dispersal was a bar where the low-minded would go and look for a fight. At least in these situation the confrontation became *mano-a-mano* but the internet is populated by cowards who hide behind screen names in a realm where there is virtually no punishment for any crime against humanity that they might commit.

But, why do people embrace anger at all? Why do they not attempt to identify the source of the anger they are feeling and then learn a method to combat the negative hold it has on their life? There are two primary reason for this: One, the person is mentally lazy and is not aware enough to realize the negative effects their anger driven mindset is having on their own life and, thus, they do not care about the repercussions that their negativity is unleashing out to the world. Two, they become addicted to the adrenaline that is realized in their body when they are overtaken by their anger. From these two reasons, the individual who is controlled by anger does not take the time to learn methods of anger management.

Anger is an emotion motivated by a person deciding to feel a certain way. Anger is not a universal emotion. It is one person deciding to feel one way about one thing. This anger is wholly motivated by the mind of one individual. Yes, others may join into and embrace one person's anger but they are simply following the pathway created by an undisciplined, uncontrolled mind. Thus, they actually become less than than the person who instigated the anger motivated moment because they are only following in someone else's anger.

Have you ever watched a person who is locked into a state of anger raging out of control? Have you ever been that person? In either case, you witness that there is a person completely out of control. From this, all kinds of damage is unleashed out to the world. And, as stated, the internet is a place where a person can go into a rage and pay no price for the words and the actions they unleash. It is not a bar fight so no one is going to punch back. If someone does do an internet punch back, all the person has to do is change their screen name and they are clean and clear. Again, this is a coward's passion and poison. For a screen name is nothing—it is a non entity. It is a coward's way to hide who and what they truly are to the world. If they were not a coward they would tell the world who they are, what they are, spell out why they are feeling the way they are feeling, and then explain to the world (and to themselves) why they do not possess the mental aptitude to actual control their anger and not let it emulate outside of themselves.

Life is a place inhabited by all of us. The internet is a place of shadows. Since the dawning of the internet religious soothsayers have said the internet is, *"The devil's tool—the devil's playground."* Yes, it is. Because no-one is anything. They are there but they are not there. They are hidden behind the veil of illusion. But, the life of the actualized, the spiritual, the enlightened, the self-aware, and the in-control person does not have to be defined like this— even on the internet. The true person, the good person does not have to fall prey to the hidden illusions and misplaced, misdirected, and uncontrolled emotions that are unleashed on the internet. You can be there without being that.

Ultimately, life comes down to who you are, what you experience, how you react to those experiences, and what you are willing to do about controlling who and what you actually are and what you present to the world.

The fact is, your emotions do not matter. They do not matter to anyone but you. If you are motivated by your emotions to make judgments, present untruth, half truths, say bad things, do bad things, and act in an unenlightened manner, then all that does is define who you truly are. And, if you behave in this manner, that who you are is not a good thing. If you broadcast your emotion-based judgments out to the world, damaging any-one, any-thing, or the positivity of the world in general, do you actually believe that at some point in your life you will not be held responsible? And, this is the thing about the internet, people think they can away with saying or doing anything. Though that one action, that one word, that one burst of anger may get to be written and sent out in the world of cyberspace, if you do not learn to control your anger and your negative emotions, if you do not own your anger and repair any damage you may have unleashed because of that anger, all your life will be defined by is that you were a coward who was not brave enough to even reveal who you truly are and why you did not have enough self-control to control the judgments, the lies, and anger they unleashed onto the world.

Own you anger. Fix your anger. Make the world a better place.

When You Ain't Got Nothing Else to Talk About
18/Jan/2017 09:29 AM

    I forever find it interesting when I am sitting around somewhere: at a restaurant, a bar, a coffee house or something and I hear people out of nowhere discussing sports. Here are two (or more) people, who live in completely different worlds, have completely different lifestyles, and totally different life interests but there they are talking sport. They are discussing how this team should do that, this player needs to work on his game, how that team has no chance of making it to the playoffs, etc., etc., etc… Totally different people, with absolutely nothing in common, talking sports—sometimes arguing sports.

    For me, who has very little interest in team sports, I find these discussions amusing. Sometimes people try to draw me into their sport's talk but I always joking tell them, *"I am way too self involved to be into sports."* I love to play sports but talking about others playing sports, it is just not my thing.

    But, this all goes to an interesting byproduct of modern civilization and the psychology of the human being… People want to communicate. People want to have interaction. People want to be heard. And, for those who no one is listening to, the discussion of sports is a way to cross all kinds of socioeconomic and personality gaps and find a common ground.

    Certainly, most sport's talk is limited to men. But occasionally, you find a woman who knows the game(s). But, when men approach women to, *"Talk,"* the focus of that conversation generally seems to hold a difference set of definitions.

    The problem with sport's talk and, in fact, with talking about anything, *"Out there,"* is that a person has no control onto what is actually happening. These armchair quarterbacks can talk and talk, voice their opinions, but that is all that it is, *"Opinion."* Their words are not based in fact or upon anything that has any chance of changing or altering anything. They are just speaking words that are lost to the cosmos; equaling nothing.

Some people spend their entire life speaking about others. If it is not sports, it is expressing their opinions about other people doing other things. But, they are not the person, they have never lived the life of that person, they were not there when that person did whatever it is they did. So, in fact, they have no true knowledge about anything to do with that person or with that person's life or their creations or accomplishments.

Here is the place where people's lives go astray. They live through other people. As they talk about other people, they think about other people. They may love that person, they may hate that person, they may honor that person, they may believe they know that person's personal history, they may even judge that person and/or all other people but all any of this equals is talking about other people. It never equals personal enlightenment. It never equals personal accomplishment. In only equals talk. And talk, equals nothing but talk.

So, this is question(s) you have to ask yourself whenever you find yourself talking about something or someone out there, *"Why am I even thinking about them?" "Why am I not doing something with my own life instead of talking about what someone else has done with their life?"*

Your life begins and ends with what you do. If all you do is talk about someone else; believing that you know them, thinking that you know what they have experienced, thinking that you understand why they do what they do, telling other people this person's life history, and thinking you know about what they should do next, your life will end empty with you having accomplished nothing. As long as you talk, you do not do. Stop talking and live. Stop talking and create.

Do Something Special Every Day
17/Jan/2017 04:23 PM

Life goes by in the blink of an eye. When you are young you don't think about this. When you are old it is too late to think about this. One day you are young; the next day years have gone by but you never saw them going. You never see the passing of time until that time has past. You can only look back and remember your life experiences. Yes, during your life there are good times and there are bad times but while you are living them, you are locked into them. Thus, they are only judged through the passage of time.

Many people choose to live a very mundane existence. The do the same thing everyday. Some like what they do and they are content in their mundane. That is a good thing. Most people, however, are not like this. And, that is bad thing.

Many people feel trapped by their life-definitions. They feel they must do what they must do. But, if what they must do brings them no joy, their entire life passes by with not only a sense of angst and regret but also with a longing to have lived something else. From this is born all of the internal anger perpetuated out to the world by the words and the deeds of the unhappy and the unfulfilled individual.

For many, their life is defined by a sense of necessity. They must do what they must do to survive and/or to feed their family. Again, this goes back to the core principle of life; some people love or at least accept the cards life has dealt them; making the best out of them, while others are regretful and become bitter and angry.

Though there are spiritually based metaphysical methods to teach a person how to rethink and reencounter their life; this takes training. A training that many do not wish to undergo. Thus, what can a person do if they find that they are living a life that they wish was different? The answer, *"Do something special everyday."*

Many people adequate, *"Special,"* with something big. A trip to Hawaii, a new car, a new lover, a new and better job. But, *"Special,"* doesn't have to be that. Special can be something very small but very personal. If you like to take a walk, take a walk everyday. Go have a cappuccino. Join a gym. You never know who you will meet. Take a class in something that you are interested in. Go do some hatha yoga. You name it… Special is anything that takes you away from the forced and the mundane in your life. Special is anything that takes your mind off of all the stuff you normally think about. Special is something that makes you feel special. Special does not have to cost money. Special is taking a moment, talking yourself out of any drudgery that you may be encountering, and altering you mind to a place where new and happy realization and life experiences may be born.

Do something special every day.

You Just Can't Talk About Nothing to No One
15/Jan/2017 08:41 AM

Each of us has our private thoughts, ideas, and life experiences that we wish to keep to ourselves. Maybe we only share them with someone close to us who either experienced those moments with us or someone we feel very close to. Certainly, in this modern world, people spread all kinds of everything about themselves out to the world via social media. In times gone past, this was not the case. There was no social media. And, in a lot of ways this was better. One's life and one's life experiences was kept to themselves. From this, a deeper understanding of one's life was possible as it was personally thought about as it was individually studied. Now, everything is blurted out to the world and then forgotten. Freeing, maybe… But, also damning, as what one thinks, feels, and experiences is told to people who do not truly care about that person. Then what? From this, all kinds of chaos can be unleashed.

Have you ever told someone a secret and they told it to other people? Have you ever told someone, whom you were very close to, something very personal, then your relationship went downhill and they used it as a tool against you? Hopefully, none of this has happened to you. But, for many of us, it has. And, this is not good. If you can't trust the people who are close to you or who once were close to you, who can you trust?

Most people are very self motivated. They only care about another person as long as they care about that person. This caring can be based in many factors but this caring is almost always dominated by a personal end-goal; i.e., getting what they want from a person be it friendship, guidance, love, sex, money, you name it…

It is sad but it is true; very few people simply care about a person to care about them. Sadder still is the fact that most people never even think about caring about someone they do not know. Most, do not have the capacity to care about someone out there in the ethos—out there in the world beyond the realm of, *"I personally know you."*

Lack of caring and self motived life living is what causes people to take what a person has told them, break their confidence, and tell it to others. This is also the causation factor for people to alter the actual life experiences that have occurred with a specific person and then repeat those life experiences, via an altered state, to other people who have no need in knowing them.

Have you ever had that happen to you? Have you ever befriended someone; maybe you liked them, maybe you tried to help them, maybe you let them into your life, and then they became dissatisfied or angry at you, (for who knows what self motivated reason), and then they took all that you did for them, added a negative spin to it, and spread it out to the world via an untruthful, negative storyline? I have.

Do the people who do this truly care about you? No. Do the people who spread your secrets truly care about you? No. They only care about themselves, how they are feeling, and if they are getting what they want from a specific individual. This is a very low state of consciousness but it is the state that many, if not most, people embrace.

You can look at a person's life and you can see by the way they behave, where they are in their life at what age, what they do for a living, and what they are setting up for their future, who they truly are—whether they have lived a life of good intend or ill will. But, many people, seeing who a person is, still attempt to help; believing that the person can become more, no matter who they are and/or were. Some people care. This is certainly one of my major faults in life. I believe in people. But, people are a cruel breed. Look around you. Look at the people you have encountered. Look at the people who have taken your confidence and used it to negative ends.

Now, one could look at their life, their life interactions with other people, and their life experiences and run away from the world. Many have... Though that is probably not the best thing to do. Most people, as they pass through life, encounter those who possess a less than ideal and trustworthy mindset, deal with any havoc they may unleashed on their life, and then move away from them. The fact is, this is life and you are not going to encounter only good and caring people. You will encounter those of low mind. And, if you are not careful, you may be sucked into the life dilemma of these people.

To this end, and to get back to the primary premise of this discussion, you really need to think about whom you tell what. ...You really need to protect yourself for you never know what someone has the potential to unleash on you once they know your secrets.

If you have no secrets, you are all good. If you don't care that everyone knows everything, again, you are all good. But, this is rarely the case with anyone's life. Secrets are what keeps the life of someone else a mystery. And, without mystery, all the illusion fades away.

Is Doing What You Do Okay As Long As You Don't Get Caught?
14/Jan/2017 07:42 AM

There is this video that has been circulating around Facebook and I imagine other places that shows Neil Young going into a record store in the 1970s, getting upset that they are selling a bootlegged record of one of Crosby, Stills, Nash, and Young's concerts, telling the young cashier (who has no idea who he is) that they can't sell that record as he wrote the songs, giving him his contact info to give to his boss, and walking out the door with it. From a filmmaking perspective it is not shot very well but it was obviously done on a 16mm camera and the audio is really good so they obviously had a sound guy in tow. Meaning, this encounter was totally set up. Why? I do not know. Maybe Young was planning to use it in a film? Maybe it did?

Overall, it is a bit painful to watch as it is long and drug out. The cashier chases Young out to the street. ...Can't blame the kid for that... You can see where the camera man had to change his mag as four-hundred foot loads only shoot for twelve minutes. Finally, it ends with Young going back into the store, talking to the owner on the phone, and leaving with the record after not paying for it.

Okay... What does all this tell us about life? First of all, if I was Neil Young I probably would have just paid for the record and left behind all of the melodrama. I'm sure he had the money. But, on the other side of the issue, I totally get it. In this modern digital age, people steal my creative work from me all time. People watch my movies for free from illegal download sites, read my books, and download my music. Though me, the creator, is not getting paid, the people who have stolen my stuff are getting paid or they would not be doing it. Just as is the case of the people who recorded, pressed, and released bootleg records back in the day—they wouldn't be doing it if they weren't getting paid.

In the modern world, very few people ever think about any of this. As they are not creating anything, they don't care. At best, they hope to create something someday… But, someday never comes. Thus, they take from the lives and the bank accounts of those who do create and they do not care.
…They do this because they will never be caught.

I believe most people would not go into a store and actually steal a DVD, a CD, or anything like that. But, stealing on the internet… They never even ponded the overall consequences of their actions. As long as they get away with it, they don't care.

Growing up on the wrong side of the tracks as it were, in my early years, I knew a lot of seedy people who did some very bad things. Luckily, my mind was focused on other things and I never went down that path. But, they would be all proud and bragging about what they did. They were proud and bragging until they got caught and ended up in jail. And, we all know what happens there. Some, I never heard from again.

In my adult years, I have known a few people were drug dealers. They all thought it was a cool way to make money while staying high. One friend of mine ending doing five and half years in an Arizona prison. He got out and died a few years later. Was it worth it? Losing your life-time?

People who are in the game of taking for free never think about any of this until they are forced to think about it. Though I doubt the law(s) will ever focus very prominently on people who rob people's livelihood by stealing their creations via the internet, you as a thinking person should be more than that. You should decide that simply because you will not be caught and held to task, that does not mean that it is okay to steal.

The good in all life begins with you deciding to do the right thing. The bad in all life also begins with you deciding to do the wrong thing. Thus, you are the source for all that is good and/or bad.

If you see something bad, you should call it out. You should tell the person to stop. You should make it stop. You should try to replace and fix anything bad that was done by doing something good.

You know what is good or bad. You know what is right or wrong. Choose to only do good, stop allowing other people to be hurt by people who do bad things just because they won't be caught. Make the world a better place.

The First Time I Was Lied To
13/Jan/2017 07:46 AM

I've noticed that recently whenever I turn on a program on TV or pull up a movie on-demand that someone will be giving somebody their music demo CD. This sets me thinking…

Back in the 1970s when the personal 4-Track Reel-to-Reel Recorders were released I was one of the first to buy one. They were great! For the first time, multi-instrumental musicians like myself or bands could actually record their own music via multi-track performances and actually create a fully orchestrated presentation. Certainly, they were no where near what can be done today on your PC but they were the first step in true home recording.

I was in my early semesters at college and I met a girl in one of my classes. We got to talking, hung out a bit, and she told me that she knew some music producer who was looking for a new performer. I guess it was due to the fact that I had grown up in Hollywood and had interacted with a lot of people who were actually family members of some really high-end people in the film and music business that I didn't doubt what she told me. I bought into it… With this, I set about creating a demo tape in my apartment.

I was totally focused and totally in a state of belief that this could be my ticket. As anyone who is a young musician (or once was a young musician) understands, there are all the dreams of musical stardom. From this, I became highly focused and recorded the demo tape. I mixed it and gave it to her on cassette…

After that, though I would see her around campus, it seemed like she was avoiding me. Finally, I needed to know what was up. As it turned out, the only person she knew, who had anything to the with the music industry at all, was her ex-boyfriend who was in band and he didn't like my demo tape. Of course not. But, would have gone through all that time, focus, energy, and process to create a tape for a guy in a post-high school hard rock band? Hell no! I got pulled into the lie.

Now, the fact of life is, some people lie all the time. But, why? Mostly, they lie because they want to seem like something more than they actually are. They tell lies so people like me (back then) will believing them that they are something more than nothing. But, what is the desired end? I don't know… I guess each person has their own definition or undefined reasoning. But, a lie is just a lie. All a lie does is to mess with someone's life. And, that is never a good thing.

As I have long detailed, *"The number one rule of filmmaking is that everybody lies."* Lying is so rampant in the film industry that it is almost unfathomable. But, you almost expect that. A bunch of bullshit, self-involved people trying to climb up or stay on top of the heap. But, that is the film industry. In life, why do people need to lie?

I guess it really comes down to lacking a defined sense of self. If a person, no matter who they, where they came from, or what they are doing, is not whole and complete onto themselves then they may find a reason to lie as they wish to appear to be something more/something else. If they accept who they are, however, then there is no need to lie about anything.

I can tell you not to lie as it is not good and it messes not only with other people's lives but with your life, as well. …If you are found out to be a liar than a liar is all you will ever be. I can tell you this, but if you are a lair you will still lie. It is a pathology that some people develop and never get past.

But, lying is bad. Be who and what you are—whole onto yourself. Accept who you are. Be proud of who you are.

Don't lie.

Conscious Activity in an Unconscious World
12/Jan/2017 12:56 PM

It was a rainy day in L.A. and I decided to go have breakfast at this restaurant I frequent. I should preface this by stating that normally I love driving in the rain. Put on some good music, turn the windshield wipers on, and I am all good. I think it is a great experience.

Anyway, I live on this hill so to get to the main city section where the restaurant is I drive a couple of miles down this two lane street and then turn left to drive the few miles off of the hill.

So, I get in my car, turn on the tunes, head out to the street, and start to drive. Up near the intersection when I need to turn, I have to get over to the left lane. I was driving in the slow lane and another car, a Porsche Boxster, was in the passing lane; driving parallel to me. But, I had to get over. I slow down, they slow down. I speed up, they speed up. In doing this, they completely kept me from getting into the lane where I needed to be in. Had this been in any other type of circumstance, I would have assumed the driver of the other car was just fucking with me but I could see it was just some lady not paying attention. As she was not paying attention, she was driving in zombie mode. Any car around her (i.e., mine) slows down, she slows down. Any car around her speeds up, she speeds up.

Have you ever ridden with a person who drives like this? I have and it drives me nuts. I want to scream. They get behind a car on the freeway and no matter how fast or slow that car goes, they just play follow-the-leader. That is really a bad driving habit.

Finally, I step on the gas and speed up and turn in ahead of her. I turn left and begin to go down the hill. But, there again, there she is; riding right next to me. This time, to my right, in the slow lane.

As we approach this intersection, a cop has just turned his roof lights on as he wants to make a U-turn where normally one is not allowed. But, he's a cop... This all happened very quickly and due to the fact that the road was wet I did not want to slam on my breaks and slide through the intersection. Especially with a cop right there. So, I gradually slowed down and tried to pull over to the side. As I did, the lady in her Porsche was right there—right next to me. As I tried to pull over, at whatever speed I attempted, she was there keeping me from getting to the curb. I was simply in disbelief. I wanted to yell at her but I knew she wouldn't hear me. Finally, I got over, and the cop passed by.

After the cop passes, I pull out and the drive is back on. Shortly ahead, the cop stopped in the middle of one lane but then waved the traffic on around him. This time, to keep from having to deal, I let the lady in her Porsche go first. Up ahead was a minor fender-bender. Sure, you're suppose to go slow around those, especially on a rainy day. But, the lady in her Boxster completely stopped right next to the accident—I guess to study the crash. When she saw enough, only then did she drive on. By this point, I was just so annoyed...

Do people not even consider that there are other people in the world—that what they are doing is affecting those other people? I guess not.

In any case, I ate breakfast and set out to a pre-production meeting I was to have regarding an upcoming project I am set to do in Reykjavik in the Spring. As I was a little early, I stopped off at this vintage clothing boutique that I go to sometimes. I was shopping...

The aisles in this shop tend to be fairly tight as it is a pretty small place. For example, the men's pants are on one side of an aisle and the women's are directly across from it. There is only maybe three feet in between. I was looking in that aisle and a woman is there with her shopping cart. I'm looking through the pants and she pushes her cart into my leg. No bid deal. I just thought it was just a mistake. She does it again, I say nothing. The third time she pushes it into me with some force. Finally, I say, *"Are you just gong to keep pushing your cart into my leg?"* Her answer, *"I want to look down this aisle and you are in my way."* Are you fucking kidding me? I couldn't even believe what she just said.

Now, what does all this tell us about life? Some people are so unconscious about the impact they are having on others and/or some people just don't care about what they are unleashing. All they think about is themselves and in some cases, they are thinking about nothing at all. But, what they do does have an impact—it unleashes a negative experience onto the lives others. But, do they care? Probably not. They are so locked into their own self-absorbed mind and their own meaningless momentary reality that they do not even consider the impact they are having on others. They do not care what they are unleashing. How about you? Do you act like this?

If you don't think about other people first you have no right to do anything in this world.

The true definition of a human being is someone who cares and thinks about the impact they are having before that impact is ever encountered by anyone else.

High Mind, Low Mind, and the Road to Success
12/Jan/2017 08:34 AM

I was watching an episode of a Reality TV Show the other night. The cast was a sitting around a table talking about their dysfunctional relationships as all Reality TV Shows tend to do. All of a sudden I notice that one of the people had brought this media figure who rose to prominence, here in L.A., during the 1960s and 1970s. I was totally surprised to see him. I had not even thought about him in years and assumed he was probably dead. Out of nowhere, he pushed his way into the conversation and began spouting some regurgitated spiritual mumbo-jumbo, stolen from the mouth of some other self-help guru. You could witness the self-involved, all-knowing blankness in his facial expression and his sense of self-worth that he had something to say that he believed others needed to hear. In other words, he was nothing more that an arrogant self-involved asshole speaking something he did not truly understand that no one else, but himself, wanted to hear.

As all the people who make up this show are supremely successful; i.e. very rich, they all rolled their eyes. But, that did not take away this man's sense of self-worth, nor did it silence him.

Have you ever encountered a person like this? Somebody who thinks that they know and thinks that what they know you should hear even when you don't want to hear it? This is the sign of a low mind. But, I will get into that in moment.

After seeing this guy, and being reminded of his existence, I decided to look him up on the good old, inter-web. I mean, you can find the bio and/or possibly interviews of anyone of substance on the web; right?

I found stuff… Yes, as I remembered, he first did early versions of what may be described as MTV style music interview shows on PBS, here in L.A., back in the 60s and into the 70s. He then was an entertainment correspondent on a network news show here in L.A. and finally he went onto being a radio DJ for a time. All remember... As a kid and a teenager, I though he was pretty cool as he had long hair and was rock'n it on TV. I remember I even called in and talked to him about Macrobiotics (which I was totally into at one point) when he was doing a radio talk show. Though then, as now, I thought he was pretty arrogant in his response, I did get my point across. I also found an interview with him on the net. Surprisingly, he described himself as someone who took more than five years to finish high school. Back in a time when high school was only three years. And, he said his IQ was ten points below the average. As he put it, *"I'm not very smart."* Wow... Not very smart, yet he was so successful. How does that happen?

Reading this, I was very so surprised that someone/anyone would spread that fact to the world. How very self-actualized.

But, that comment made me think to my own life and how, due to the fact that I did very well in school, I was given a couple of IQ tests in grammar school. As it turned out, my IQ was very high and they wanted to put me in advanced programs. But, my parents, being far more focused upon their careers than their kid, thought that keeping me in public school was good enough. As my young life progressed and through a process of life events and experiences I very consciously decided that school was a bunch of BS and why should I even care enough to care. Thus, I became a very bad student. None-the-less, due to the fact that I was still getting fairly high grades, (without ever trying), I was again tested in high school; same results. During my university years, I was hanging with some psych grad students and again I was tested. Though I was surprised, my IQ number had actually gone up. This, post all the drugs, all the living life on the edge, and a motorcycle accident that fractured my brain. But, as I have questioned throughout my life, what does an IQ number matter? I always felt that there was a lot of people a lot smarter than me not getting tested. What does an IQ number actually tell you? In my life, I have encountered some people that were very smart. I have also encountered some very brain-dead people. They all passed from birth to death doing what they did. Yet, here was a guy who labeled himself as not very smart having become very successful. But, was there something missing in this equation?

Have you ever sat down with a person who puts on a set of headphones and even though there is no music or words playing through them they began to speak very loudly? They are compensating for themselves not hearing their own words in the same manner as without the headphones. I have noticed this phenomenon ever since I was a young kid. To me, that was always the definition of someone who was not very smart. (Donald G. Jackson did this all the time). The average person, understanding that they have headphones on, adapts their mind and the volume of their voice. Others do not. But, what does this tell us about a person and their level of interactive intelligence? It tells us that they are so locked into their own mindscape that they are not self-aware and/or intelligent enough to adapt to the world around them. They are locked in their own perception of reality and the way they want that reality to be broadcast to the world. They want to hear themselves be heard.

Now, I could go into the discourse I commonly details about the level of bullshit that is employed by all of the people who speak out about spirituality and how they believe one should encounter life. ...People who have never been a disciple—people who have never lived a truly spiritual life—never earned an advanced degree in psychology or sociology or anything... So, they have no true bases to say anything. Then, on the other side of the coin, there was someone like Leonard Cohen (who we recently lost) who lived in a monastery for several years; he had the right to speak but he did not. The knowers know in their silence. They do not need to speak. The speakers want to be heard and they want to be acknowledged even if what they are saying is not based upon empirical knowledge—it is only based upon what I like to call, *"Borrowed knowledge."*

And, I guess this takes us to the point of all this… Success is not based upon an IQ number. It is not based upon whether a person is smart or dumb. Success is based upon inter-personal drive. It is based upon a defined sense of self-sensationalism that drives a person forward to a level where someone else will listen to them even if no one wants to hear what they have to say.

Who are you? What do you do in life? What do you say in life? Do the people that are around you want to hear what you have to say? Or, are you so self-involved that all you do is to speak when no one is listening?

Though success is based in drive, true life contribution is based upon self-revealed revelations. Do you speak your realizations or do you copy the words of others just so people will look to you as someone who know? …Making yourself feel important when no one else really cares who or what you truly are?

Let Your Freak Flag Fly
11/Jan/2017 07:42 AM

For those of us who came of age during the 1960s and to a lesser degree during the 1970s we understand how much a man with long hair was looked down upon. And, it didn't have to be that long—just an inch or two over the ears and one had, *"Long hair."* All kinds of negative things occurred from that. People yelled things. When the cops arrested someone they often chopped off the guy's locks. You couldn't even get into Disneyland if you were a guy with long hair.

In one's teen years, when many a young man gets his first job, many/most places would not even hire a man unless they had short hair. This was even true of those who worked for Yosemite and I imagine other National Parks. Even my contemporaries at Hollywood High School, a place where one may believe that a person would be surround by a more accepting world, you could always tell the guy who had a, *"Job,"* as they had short hair.

One guy I knew really impressed me. If you would see him at school, he had long hair. But, if you went into the local Vons Supermarket, it looked like he had short hair. I asked him about this and he told me how his mother and him had concocted a method to bobby pin his hair up so it looked short. I thought this was a great way to beat the system. I'm sure he went far in life.

Overall, I always thought this was a strange way to judge a person—by the length of their hair. I mean, it was only a generation or two the previous where long hair on a man was completely accepted.

On a personal note, from my early years forward I was always very identified with the counter culture. As such, I had long hair. When I was about thirteen, my mother, being from a different generation, and hating long hair on men, wanted me to cut it. I refused. So, one night, while I was asleep, she came in and cut it off. I woke up to a pillow full of my hair. As you can imagine, I was very upset as it was part and parcel of who I was back then. I'm sure you remember how important things like that were when you were a teenager… Me, I've never really sleep well since that experience. But, that just lets you know the level of hatred and social stigma that was focused towards men with long hair.

Anyway, as the days of the hippies waned, people began to refer to men with long hair as, *"Freaks."* Those of us who had long hair, during that era, embraced this term and we began referring to ourselves as, *"Freak."* From this was born the term, *"Let your freak flag fly."* Meaning, grow your hair out and embrace the unaccepted.

As time has gone on, certainly long hair on men became more and more accepted. At the point celebrities began growing their hair long it infiltrated and became accepted within modern culture. Now, a man with long hair may be noticed and perhaps defined by it but this does not keep them from obtaining employment, drawing outside criticism, or anything like that.

All this being said, hair is a great thing. It's beautiful. Letting your hair grow is a great thing. And, this is true for both men and women. Though you are certainly no longer making a counter culture statement by growing your hair long, you are making a statement about accepting the free and the natural—you are making a statement about being your own person.

So, I say, *"Let your freak flag fly."* Take a year, two, or three and let your hair grow. It will open up a whole new level of reality for you.

To What End?
10/Jan/2017 08:03 AM

Most people spend very little time contemplating what they are doing and why. They just DO. And, this DOING is not done in the conscious/unconsciousness of Zen. It is just reactionary life-babble launched out to the world with no pre-thought. It is just DONE.

But, if you DO with no thought of your DOING, if you DO without knowing why you DO, your life passes by and all you have to show for it is what was DONE by you. You wake up at the end of your life and question what any of it meant.

Conscious living is based in consciousness. Unconscious living is based upon a reactionary mindset compelled by desire, wanting, longing, and anger at what you do not have.

Some people happily pass unconsciously through their life. Their needs are mostly met so they go from birth to death with a smile on their face. This is rare, however. Most people who live their life, based upon not-thinking, are driven more by the negative emotions than the positive. They love, they hate, they want, they desire, they react, and/or overreact to all that they experience and thus, from this, they hurt. Hurting anyone for any reason is never a good thing.

But, as most people do not even ponder why they are doing what they are doing, what can you do? All you can do is know your WHY. All you can do is look to yourself, study your reality, come to understand your WHY and know why you are doing what you are doing.

We all do. Each day we each develop a ritual. We wake up and set about on a specified course of action and reaction. This is natural. Do what you do. That is life. But, with each step you take, each action you make, ask yourself why you do what you do and what does that action give to you, your life, your family, and the world around you.

Knowing YOU is the key component to not only understanding life and making YOUR life a better experience but it is also the key to making the overall world a better place.

The Road to Stardom
08/Jan/2017 02:53 PM

As some of you may or may not know, I'm on the voting board for SAG/AFTRA. So, when award's season comes around I'm given a lot of screener copies of the movies that are in contention. Last night I sat down and watched *La La Land.*

Before I go into all this, I think I should say that *La La Land* is not the kind of movie I would normally watch—a little too much of a Chick Flick for my tastes. Plus, I've never really been a fan of musicals—even when they were grand with the likes of Gene Kelly and Fred Astaire. …Though the original Grease was pretty good. But, as I am going to have to vote for or against the film I felt it was my obligation to watch it.

The film was what the film was… The problem I had with it, and a lot of other films of this nature, is that it focuses on people who come to Hollywood, struggle, and then eventually emerge as major stars. I truly believe that this is the wrong message to send. It just doesn't happen! Sure, there is the story of this person or that who came to Hollywood and, *"Made it."* From this, so many people believe that it will also be them. Movies like La La Land feed into this belief. But, for every person who has made it, millions have not. And, of the few who do, *"Make it,"* for a moment, they eventually fall from grace and then what happens to them?

As someone who grew up in Hollywood, I saw this all around me. Even many of the so called, *"Famous,"* people I encountered when I was young were constantly broke and doing anything it took just to get by as they hoped, dreamed, and schemed of their next role. I remember when Donald G. Jackson and I went to ask the Great Hollywood Bad Guy, William Smith, who had been in tons and tons of films and even co-starred with Clint Eastwood, to be in the

Roller Blade Seven, he literally cried as he was so thankful to be offered a role as he had no money and was just couch surfing from friend to friend.

Then, there are also the majority of the dreamers—those who come here, don't make it, and end up as hookers or junkies and homeless. Stardom, it just does not happen!

As a filmmaker, and I have said this many times before, the reason I forever reach out to the unknowns for my cast is that I hope to give these people at least a little bit of something to show for their time here in Hollywood. ...A role that they can send home to their family and say, *"Look at me. I'm in a film."* Because this does not happen for most. Sure, being an extra is easy. Almost anybody can do it. But, getting an actual role, it does not happen for the vast majority of all those who travel to Hollywood. At least some have families to go back home to. That is good. For if you don't, then what will happen to you?

There is a lot of hype about *La La Land* and I am sure it will win at lot of awards this season. I'm not going to vote for it. But, that's just me. Why? Because I think that its message is very dangerous.

It's essential to remember, if you're setting your site on Hollywood, always have a safety net—don't go All-In. Because life is not like the movies. You are not going to become a star.

The Race of the Family
07/Jan/2017 08:49 AM

Family connection are an integral part of life. When you study people who have a large direct and extended family you truly see how their interactions with their family sets the stage for their entire life. Yes, they may totally love or hate one particular family member, judge, make fun of, and look down upon another, but as a cohesive whole that family unit extends throughout their entire life. They spend their life interacting with these people. When they need companionship, support (financial or otherwise), help, to not be alone, you name it, they turn to their family. This is what family is for.

In some cases, people develop a family outside of their own bloodline. This can happen via a religious group, when someone is in combat, or maybe a gang for a street kid. Though these people are not an actual family, some people turn to these external groups in order to fill a void in their life if their actual family is unavailable.

Those people who make up this pseudo-family may, in fact, provide some of the same elements of interactive family consciousness but there is, in most cases, a big difference between these groups in that they are not blood—they have no necessity to love, care for, and/or help a person if they go astray from what is expected of them. If a person does something that is considered wrong, in most cases, they are sent packing. A true family, however, a family made up of bloodline, is far more forgiving. They tend to forgive, try to understand, and try to help anyone within their clan that may have done something wrong. And, this is a good thing.

Family is an essential element of life. There is the family we are born into and then there is the family we become a part of. This takes place through marriage and/or cohabitation. But, this is a complicated relationship. I think for any of us who has met someone, fallen in love, and began to hang out with that person is association with their family, we can attest to the fact that at the outset there is always a lot of trepidation directed towards us. *"Are we good enough?" "Will we treat the family member right?"* In some cases, this all works out and two family units merge. But, to what degree? Do they ever become one whole? I think not. This is especially the case when two specific family units are not of the same race or not from the same culture.

Race and culture forever places a vast variable into any equitation. Yes, yes, in the not too far off future there will only be one race. But, that is still not now. So today, race plays a part in everything. Not only in the question asked if a person is good enough, but also, *"What will that person, of a different race or culture, bring to our family?"*

From my own personal perspective, I have seen this very clearly. One Caucasian man is responsible for bringing the entire family and extended family of my lady from their native Korea. Though they all owe him their entire existence here in the United States, as do all the following generations that were born due to the marriages and the procreation of these people, when it was time to give him something the family divided and many of them turned their backs to him. All based on bloodline and race. Sure, he's invited to family dinners and stuff but that is just lip service at best, for when it comes down to the all and the everything he is not one of them. Me too... Though a spouse may have a different perspective, the extended family sticks to their own. Not necessarily right, but that is what family does. I have witnessed this within this same family when new family members of Korean descent entered the fold and they were heartily embraced, when a Caucasian came on board, not so much...

I look to my own family structure and I basically have none. My aunt and uncle, on my mother's side, never married so they had no children. When my father passed away, when I was a young boy, I never saw any of his family again. So, I had virtually no direct or indirect extended family. This caused me to develop a sense of (for lack of a better word) isolationism. But, it also gave me the ability to truly look into the family structure due to the fact that it was so alien to me.

Family members, particular family members of a direct bloodline, form one cohesive whole. They are of one-mind when it comes time to require one-mind. A family possessing one-mind is always greater than one person thinking one thing—whatever that one thing may be. The key to a good, whole, protected, and productive life, embrace your family. If not, you are all alone. And thought, *"All alone,"* may sound poetic and/or spiritual it is not.

What Do You Give Me?
06/Jan/2017 07:42 AM

The world is in a constant state of give and take. Most people want to take—they want what they want when they want it and they want it for free and the consequence to the lives of other people be damned. Most people do not want to give. In fact, they rarely think about giving. Sure, they know when it is Christmas they must buy their family or friends Christmas presents. But, that is forced giving. That is not true giving.

Giving is giving because you care about a person—because you want to make their life better. You may have to go out of your own way to do it—you may have to work hard to give the gift (whatever that gift may be) but you are willing to do it because you want to give, you want to make another person's world a better place.

How often do you give when you are not required to do so? How often do you even think about giving? How much of your Life-Time do you actually spend thinking about other people, instead of only thinking about yourself and set about on a course to make someone else's something better and more? The answer to those questions will tell you a lot about yourself.

I have often made the semi-joking statement when asked about realizations from my own life, *"Everybody wants something from me but nobody ever gives me anything."* I could go into the whys and wherefores, psychological or otherwise, about the reasoning behind this life conclusion but that is not really the point. It is simply my realizations about my life. I wish it were otherwise, but it is not.

Now, think about your own life. Do you find that you think about others and actually care enough to care? I'm not necessarily talking about your direct family, someone you may currently be in love with, or people like that. I am talking about people on the greater whole. Maybe someone you barely know, maybe someone you see on the street that needs a helping hand like a job or something. Maybe someone who's words or work inspires you. Do you ever give to them? Do you ever go out of your way to give to them? Do you even try? Or, do you just dismiss the thought, telling yourself that giving to them may be too hard or take too much time or energy?

If you do not try to give, that means that you are only thinking about yourself. Which equals the fact that you are a very selfish person. Are You? Do you ever think about this?

Some people give to make themselves look good. *"Oh, look at me, I give to this charity or that foundation."* That is not giving. That is self-absorption and elitism. That is egotism. That is, I have and I can give so I am better and more than you who does not give.

True giving takes the conscious mental action of actually thinking and caring about someone. It requires you to care about someone else other than yourself and for you to take the focus off of yourself. It means that instead of only wanting what you want—wanting your own life to be better, you want to make the life of someone else better. How often do you give?

People in Your Dreams
05/Jan/2017 07:37 AM

Each of us spends a good portion of our life asleep. That's just natural. When we sleep we dream. In our dreams we encounter all types of abstract realities that we have not lived here in this physical world. We also interact with people. Sometimes we dream of people we know. Sometimes we dream of people we used to know. Sometimes we dream of people we have never met. And sometimes, when we dream of people we never met, we live a scenario with them—we have a unique interaction with them—maybe we even like them and we wish that we could bring them through the walls of our dreams into reality to live what we experienced with them here and not just there.

Like the title to the old James Bond movie, *"You only live twice,"* details: you live your life and then you live in your dreams. But, I believe there are three levels to existence, not just two. There is life, there is your dreams, then there is your fantasies.

How many times have you been living a dream, perhaps with a person in your dream, then you begin to wake up? Knowing that your dream was ending and not wishing it to do so, you shifted that dream reality to fantasy as you progress to the waking state as you try to figure out how you could bring that person that has moved from your dream to your fantasy into your reality?

Dreams are an interesting thing and I believe none of us has the true answer to them. This is the thing about life, people claim that they know all kinds of things about the abstract realms of reality but that is only belief, no one truly knows. That is the great thing about life, it is all illusion; none of us ever truly know. All we can do is experience and try to come to the best conclusions that we can.

For me, ever since I was very-very young, I have studied my dreams. Perhaps, this was in large part due to the fact that when I was young I begin to dream the future. Like all people, I would dream but then, sometime in the near future, I would find that I was living that exact moment with the exact set of people that were in my dream. But, the way life played out, it would always conclude just a bit differently than it did in my dreams. As I grew older, and begin to study on the spiritual path, I concluded that the difference between life reality verse dream reality was probably based in the choices the individuals had made prior to arriving at that stage of their life. Thus, the conclusion played out a bit differently.

By the time I reached my later teen years I begin to dream the future and it would play out exactly as I had seen it. In a couple of cases, I realized something very negative was about to happen to a specific person that I was interacting with and I warned them to take a different road. Thus, saving them from what was to come. But, I did not like any of this. I did not want to know the future. I did not want to interrupt the future. I did not want to change the course of karma. So, I very consciously stopped allowing that to happen. But, I did not stop dreaming.

And, this is the thing… There is life and there are dreams. They are a part of us, an extension of us and, to whatever degree, an extension of our reality. We live. We dream. And, sometimes in our dreams we meet a person that we truly wish we could make a part of our living life. The problem is, no matter how hard we try to move them from there to here—no matter how much we want them to be with us here, no matter how hard we wish and believe that it can happen, it never seems to happen. Even though on the day after that dream you may find yourself looking around as you are out and about to see if you may actually meet them. Me, I often wonder, when I encounter a person in a dream like that, is that person on the other end of the dream, dreaming the same dream, and wishing I was a part of their reality? ☺

Life is a strange thing… We live but we never truly understand.

Who Am I?
04/Jan/2017 07:26 AM

There is a meditation technique, based in the Eastern tradition, where the meditator focuses on the question, *"Who am I?"* The reason for this is that it causes the mind to first evaluate and then reevaluate (over-and-over again) who you truly are. From this, it is believed, that veil upon veil of the thinking self is removed until the meditator emerges in a state of complete awareness have reached the root of their existence—removing all levels of ego they merge with the cosmic whole.

Each person is who they are. But, most people never take the time to truly analyze who they are and why they are doing what they do. Do you?

Most people are very reactionary to life. They are handed a set of circumstances and then they pass through their life either embracing or battling these circumstances.

Most people are told who they are. *"You are pretty, you are ugly, you are smart, you are stupid, you have the potential to be everything, or you will never amount to anything."* From this, people re-cast these judgments out to the world. Instead of moving beyond what they were told that they would be, they become what is/was expected of them—they become what they are told that they are. From this, they cast these same judgments onto others. But, where does all of this come from? It comes from the lack of understanding who you truly are.

If an individual does not take the time to seek deeply and discover their true inner-self, they rarely have the potential to become all that they could be. Thus, all that is left is the inner-turmoil of self deprecating judgment and the unleashing of that same ideology out, onto other people and the world as a whole. The more judgmental a person is, the least enlightened they are.

Do you care about who you are? Do you care about what you are? Do you care about anyone else? Do you care about the world as a whole? Do you focus your mind on the inner development of yourself? Do you always choose to say nice things and do nice things as opposed as to allowing your lower-self to guide you into doing and saying negative things, thereby spreading negativity across not only your own life but out to the world as a whole? Who are you? Why are you? Why do you do what you?

If you want to know who you are. If you want to know what you are. If you want to become all that you can become. If you want to make the world a better place, as you become a better person, you need to start asking the question, *"Who am I?"* You need to stop all the negativity. You need to get control of your self and control over your programming and your judgment—you need to become more. How do you become more? By knowing who you are.

Ask yourself…

Accusations by Strangers
04/Jan/2017 07:22 AM

Have you ever been judged by someone you never met? Has anyone ever told you that you were a liar when you were being completely true? Has anyone ever constructed an entire judgment orientate depiction of your life and they were completely wrong? Have you ever done this to someone else?

At the root of all human existence and all human interaction we must penetrate to the question of, *"Why?"* Why does someone behave in this manner? Why do they believe that your life is so important that they must focus on your life instead of living their own existence?

The answer is, it is easier to live, *"Out there,"* than to look, *"In here."* It is easier to construct falsehoods, based upon misplaced, unsubstantiated judgment of someone else than to look long and hard at what is going on within their own life. It is easier to focus their attention upon someone else so that no one will notice what is truly taking place within their own life.

Accusations by strangers… They are meaningless. Do not let them control you.

When Strange Things Happen
03/Jan/2017 03:29 PM

There is the really good beer called, *Oculto*. It has a really unique flavor due to the fact that it is brewed using tequila barrel staves. I guess it is a little too unique in that ever since its launch it has become harder and harder to find. Anyway, I found where some was being sold and I purchased a few six packs of it at this store yesterday. Then, we went and did the round and about the city—doing what people do on the New Years Day holiday.

I get home, I open my trunk to get out the beer and the other purchases that were made throughout the day. As can be expected, one of the six packs of beer had fallen over. No big deal. I reached in to grab one of the beers to put it back in its holder and BAM, it literally blew up. I guess the shaking pressure from ridding around in my trunk and all… Anyway, it blew up and that was all fine and good but when it blew up the flying glass put two really deep cuts into two of my fingers.

Life always amuses me… The happenings; whether they are good or bad always send me to wondering. There is always something new to learn…

I was bleeding pretty seriously all over the place and though I probably should have gone to the doctor and gotten stitches, I decided to handle it myself.

Later that evening, after I got the bleeding under control, my lady joking said to me, *"You see, god is punishing you for being mean to me."* She said this as earlier that morning I had said something she didn't like. I replied, *"No, it was your dark angels doing it to me. Tell them to stop it! I'm a nice guy."*

You know, this is the thing… People attach all kinds of superstitious everything to anything that happens to them. The Christian may say, *"God was telling me that I should not drink alcohol."* A Hindu may say, *"You are being served your karma for something you previously did."* A lot of people say a lot of things and they attempt to attribute their logic to all kinds of religious, karmic, and otherwise ideology. But, this is just life; shit happens. You may like what happens to you or you may not like what happens to you; but there is no attributable reasoning for any of it. Sometimes, weird shit just occurs.

You know, like Oscar Wilde said, *"Every saint has a past and every sinner has a future."* You can choose to do whatever it is you choose to do. If you choose to be good and do good things, that is a good thing. If you choose to be bad and do bad things, that is a bad thing. And yes, you will be responsible for all that you say and/or do; be it good or bad. But, bad things happen to good people just as good things happen to bad people. This is life. It is chaos. And, sometimes unexpected weird shit happens. There is no reason for it, it just happens.

Now, some people would have been upset by getting their fingers cut by a bottle of beer. Sure, it hurts. Sure, I don't like it. Sure, I wish it didn't happen as it will keep me from doing stuff for the next couple of days. But damn, what a weird experience. It was truly interesting watching it unfold.

This is life. Sometimes strange things happen.

Why You Do What You Do:
Reacting to the Reactive Mind
29/Dec/2016 08:09 AM

Do you ever ask yourself, *"Why am I doing what I am doing?"* Do you ever ponder that question at any/every stage of your life? The fact is, most people do not. They simply exist. They do what they do as they do it and they do not even give it any thought. But, is this a good way to live?

In modern spiritual circles there has always been the discussion of, *"Living in the now."* It is detailed that this is the best/the most spiritual place to exist. But, this whole ideology is a hoax. It is simply one more method where the so-called spiritual pundits pay lip service to that abstract realm of reality that is so impossible to achieve but so sought after. It is just another way to get people to listen to them talk.

Everybody lives in the now. This is especially true with the person who gives no thought to their existence and/or why they are doing what they do. So, is this a spiritual place to exist within? Probably not.

If you give your life no thought—if you do not contemplate what you are doing and why you are doing it then you are completely out of control of your life. Not only are you out of control of yourself but you have the very probable potential to hurt the life of other people while you are doing what you do and this is never a good a thing.

Let's look at a few examples… What do you do when you wake up in the morning? Do you do the same thing each day whether that be grabbing a smoke, drinking a cup of coffee, tea, or coke, taking a shower and shaving as you get ready for work, or stretching to keep your body loose and limber? Whatever it is, do you ever contemplate the WHY of what got you to this place in your life. Do you ever question why you ended up doing what you are doing?

Let's take this same concept a bit deeper. What do you feel when you wake up in the morning? Do you wake up to happy thoughts? Do you wake up ready to enter into meditation for a prescribed period of time? Or, do you wake up pissed off and angry thinking about how you hate your life; who you hate, what they did that you hate, and how you are going to get back at them?

People do things all the time from a space of unconsciousness. In fact, some people recognize that they are operating from a space of doing things unconsciously but they do it anyway. *"I smoke because I have an addictive personality." "I'm a drunk or a druggy because I come from a long line of alcoholics." "I always want to fight because I was beat by my parents as a child." "I'm a sex addict because I have low self esteem and I am looking for love." "I am prone to uncontrolled outbursts in my relationship due to the fact that I am jealous person." "I am lost to fits of anger because I am dissatisfied with my life or I have whatever mental aliment that the doctor told me I have."* Sure, this is all fine; finding an explanation for doing what you do. But, what does it mean? All you have done is give it name. You have not penetrated its source nor have you taken any responsibility for you doing what you are doing. Thus, you are not thinking about your actions at all. You are just doing them.

Personal responsibility and/or the lack thereof is especially pertinent when it comes to emotions. People do all kinds of things based upon emotions. This is especially the case when someone is unhappy with their own life and/or the actions of others. From this motivational mindset they do and they react. But, to what end? They may go out of their way to hurt someone else based on the emotion of anger but does that change anything within themselves? Does that make them a better person? Does that make their life any better? No, it does not. All it does is to perhaps give them a moment of empowerment. But, the problem is, all this style of behavior does is to cause reactions to their actions thus setting a whole world of anger, chaos, and retribution into motion. Like I always say, if you are saying something bad, if you are doing something bad, if you are hurting anyone there will be negative repercussion in your life. Maybe not today, but they will come. Then, all that has occurred, enacted by what you have done, is that you possibly made yourself feel better for a moment but this, *"Feeling better,"* will cause you further pain in the future.

This is the same with people who smoke, drink, or take drugs. ...And, we all know the outcome to the life of those who walk this path... What you are doing in a specific moment may make you feel the way you want to feel but by doing what you are doing not only are you damaging your own body and mind but you are negatively influencing the lives of all those around you. There will be a price to pay.

Do you think about this? Do you think about any of this? Do you ever take the time to look deeply within yourself a know why you are doing what you are doing or why you are feeling what you are feeling?

People also cause reactions within themselves. They do what they do and then they, themselves, react to it.

What they do sets a course of events into motion in their life. This can be positive but in many causes it is just the opposite because what they unconsciously do has the potential to damage not only their own life but the life of many others. But, they do it anyway. And, they do it without giving it a second thought. Then, that action comes back to haunt them. From this, they are again driven to a world based upon negative emotion as they re-react to what they are actually responsible for setting into motion. All their own fault but do they ever think about this? No, just like every other element of their life they do what they do with no conscious thought attached to that action—taking no responsibility for anything—no responsibility for any life event they are responsible for setting into motion.

Each thing that you do carves a metaphorical canyon in your brain. The more you do it, the deeper that canyon becomes. If what you are doing is a positive, conscious action then positivity results from this. You carve that canyon of conscious goodness deeper in your brain. From this, you continue to pass through life in a thoughtful, conscious, and good manner. But if, on the other hand, what you are doing is negative; either in action or thought, then you have carved a very deep canyon of negativity into you mind. The deeper any mental canyon is, the harder and harder it becomes to remove if and when you ever try to change or alter this life pattern.

    To this end, it is essential, if you want to live a good life that provides good things to the world and to your life as well, that you very consciously look at what you do, why you do it, and then come to be in control of what you do and who you are. For without this level of very conscious living, all you do is pass from birth to death as a reactionary element control by not only by your own undefined thoughts and emotions but by the hands of all others who walk this life place with no thought about anything, not even themselves.

    Be more. Think. Know who you are and why you are doing what you do. Once you know this, come to control this.

People Who Died
28/Dec/2016 07:18 AM

If I can borrow the title from the great Jim Carroll song, *"People Who Died,"* as we come to the end of the year of our lord 2016 I do not think that any of us can gloss over the fact that a lot of truly great and extremely influential and important people passed away this year: David Bowie, Prince, Glen Frey, Leonard Cohen, Paul Kantner, Leon Russell, Pete Burns, Vanity, Keith Emerson, Greg Lake, Merle Haggard, Maurice White, George Michaels, Robert Vaughn, Harper Lee, Muhammad Ali, Garry Marshall, Alan Thicke, Patty Duke, Alan Rickman, Florence Henderson, Gene Wilder, Carrie Fisher, and this is just the short list. I mean, these were all really influential people that changed the course of music, TV, cinema, and in some cases history. It's scary! In the time I have been living this life I have never seen a year when so much established greatness has been removed from this life place.

All life equals death… Sure, we can philosophize about that all you want. But, when it is gone it is gone. It will never come back. What they created will be created no more. It is very sad. This year we lost a lot of artistic greatness.

Gone is gone. Gate' Gate' Paragate' Parasamgate' Bodhi Svaha.

Looking at Humanity
27/Dec/2016 10:35 AM

Looking at humanity or the lack thereof all one has to do is to view the news and they will see that there are many-many bad things taking place. Whether it is the wars that are going on across the globe, the religious zealots who are killing the innocent, the female tourists being raped in India, the people who are being robbed, onto the senseless killings on the streets of our cities and towns there are a lot of bad people out there doing a lot of bad things.

Our world, our individual cultures, our clans and our clicks were all defined by violence. Defined by who could over power who. Humans are a violent animal. Look at the photos of any war zone. Ask anyone who was ever in a war zone. Talk to anyone who ever grew up in the gang ridden streets of the inner city; each of them will tell you that life is all about kill or be kill, who can over power who. This is who we are as human beings—this is what we are.

Have you ever watched when someone starts doing something bad and due to the energized rush of the crowd many people join in? Have you ever been drawn into the mob mentality whether it was in real life or in such abstract places as the internet? Why did you do it? What motivated you? Do you ever think about that?

Have you ever done or said something that you know was wrong, that you knew was going to hurt someone, but you did it anyway? Why did you do it?

Many people base their lives upon a mindset of judgment, power, control, and the intentional demeaning of others. As most people do not have the ability to stand on their own, face-to-face if you will, against whatever power or person that they do not like, they do it either by joining crowd consciousness or like a coward hidden behind the realms of a screen name. There is nothing new in any of this. This is what has been going on throughout human history in one form or another. Just look at the history of the world and it is easily discovered. There are those who are unfulfilled with and within their life, there are those who are dissatisfied with their life, there are those who feel powerless, there are those who are weak minded, there are those who are out of control of their own human emotions, and there are those who are just dark-dark souls that actually want to go out into the world and hurt people. Why do they—why does anyone behave in this manner? They behave in this manner because they have no understanding of their true self. They behave in this manner because they care about no one else but themselves. As they are not whole onto themselves, as they are not content in who and what they are, and in what they are doing with their life and how they are living it, they lash out in any way that is presented to them. The conscious person understands that this is not right but just look at the world, this is the way it is.

As this is the way it is, all you can do, as a conscious caring person, is to never be drawn into the darkness of doing bad things. You need to learn how to control your emotions and not be swayed by crowd consciousness. When there are bad words spoken or bad deeds about to be done, you need to intervene with positive words and positive actions. You need to stop the bad at its source. Sure, you may encounter blowback but what is the cost to you as a true, whole, and conscious individual if you don't encounter negativity with positivity and stop the ruination of people's lives at its source?

For anybody who is dissatisfied with their life, for anyone who is angry at themselves and is projecting that anger out to the world; instead of sitting around on your butt and wasting your time why don't you do something about it? Instead of being controlled by it, why don't you go out and consciously do something positive? There are so many things that you can do. You can go help at a homeless shelter, you can go spend time with the elderly who are all alone, you can go to a hospitable and work with the children who are dying. If you want your life to truly mean something, if you want to be more than the destruction that is unleashed by the misdirected emotions of the people who are only embracing their lower-self then stop focusing on yourself and DO SOMETHING GOOD and DO IT EVERYDAY!

NEVER be a part of the NEGATIVE. ONLY be a part of the POSITIVE.

Who's Reality is This?
AKA How You Remember Things
27/Dec/2016 07:58 AM

I was over at a family member's house about a week ago and I was totally surprised that she was drinking out of a Mickey Mouse mug with the date 2003 on the handle. The interesting thing about this was that another family member had given these mugs as Christmas gifts in 2003 and I had just been drinking coffee out of one of them that very morning. ...As I was drinking coffee that morning I was thinking how it was very interesting that this mug had survived this long as mugs usually get dropped, knocked over, and they break. But, there it was—she was drinking out of one, as well. We both still had ours 2003 Mickey Mouse mugs.

In any case, I noticed the mug and said, *"We still have ours, as well."* She then went into a whole discourse about whom had given her the mug. The problem was, she was totally wrong. She thought it was a friend of hers who gave it to her but I knew who actually gave it to her; I was there! As someone with an eidetic memory believe me when tell you, I remember everything and it is much more of a curse than an asset. But, there she was, she had a memory of a situation and a gift but she was wrong. That is not the way it happened.

Have you ever encountered a situation like that? ...Someone tells you a story about a situation you both lived but you remember it totally differently? It comes down to the question of, who is right and who is wrong—whose memory is correct and whose is incorrect? Whose reality is this?

How you remember your life is how you remember your life. How I remember my life is how I remember my life. Many people, though they know the truth about what they have lived consciously change the facts to make their life and their life experiences grander, better, or, in some cases, even less demeaning or traumatic. That is a conscious action—as questionable and misguided as that action may be.

Some people choose to alter the truth about their life-situations all the time for all kinds of reasons. I'm not talking about that here. What I am speaking about is the fact that people remember things differently. But, why do they do that? Is it that they want to have lived a situation differently than it was lived so their inner-mind alters the truth? Or, in their mind have they embellished the actuality of a situation so much that when it is re-remember and re-broadcast it comes out differently? Perhaps, as in the case of my aforementioned family member, do they simply remember it incorrectly? And, the ultimately question regarding this subject is, does it really matter?

You pass through your life collecting your memories. I pass though my life collecting my memories. At the end of the day all we have is a collection of life-memories—lived-moments that we retain. The fact is, think how much of your life you have lived that you have absolutely no cognitive memory of at all. You lived that time but it is gone. Though there may be some deep hidden places in your brain where all those lost memories are stored but unless you access that place with some super mind penetrating elixir those memories will be gone from your life forever. You only remember what you remember. But, what if you are remembering it incorrectly? If someone reminds you of the actuality of the truth does your mind reprocess, recalculate, and remember the actual lived reality? Or, are you lost to the lie of a falsely defined reality that you never re-remember the true-truth?

So, what does memory mean? It means that what you remember is what you remember. If what you remember is what actually occurred, then you remember the truth. If what you remember is not what actually happened than you are living a lie. But, what does it matter? It only matters if someone else remembers it differently. So, your reality is defined by you. It may be based upon the truth; it may be based upon a lie but it is your reality. Are you willing to question it?

Damned Throughout Eternity
26/Dec/2016 07:40 AM

Should a person who's done a bad thing be damned throughout eternity? It's an interesting question, don't you think? How do you feel about it? Should someone who did something bad to you be defined by what they did forever? Or, can they be forgiven and move on? How about you? Should you be forgiven for the bad things that you have done to other people?

I arrived at a Starbucks the other day, I sat down outside as my lady when in to grab our lattes. While I was sitting, there was a group of three young men sitting at a table near to mine. They were all taking very loudly about their time lost in the drink and the drugs. Yelling, *"Fucking,"* every other word. They loudly spoke—they loudly compared stories. It was just driving me nuts. Don't you hate it when people are just way too loud?

Anyway, one of them started to speak about how, during the time he was living in Santa Cruz, he totally jacked this guy up because he needed drugs; robbing him of all kinds of money and really messing his life up. He went on to say, *"As per the program,"* how he apologized to him. From this, he felt totally resolved.

Me, I wanted to scream—scream as loudly as they were talking, *"Yeah, but did you pay him back that money that you stole? Did you fix what you broke in his life?"* But, I stayed quiet. Finally, when my lady returned with the drinks they took the volume down a couple of notches. But, please…

How many people do how many damaging things to people lives and do nothing to repair the damage? As I see it, this is the whole problem with programs like AA and NA. It just gives people a platform to brag about all their doings. I mean, this guy was obviously proud about what he had done in the damaging of the others person's life or he would not be spouting it to the world. He would be ashamed and he would have kept it to himself.

I have observed people a lot throughout my life. I have encountered some people who have really messed with the lives of others—including mine. Over time, some of these people have bitten the dust really hard. From this, some of these people turn to religion. I see them on Facebook, and places like that, re-sending out all these spiritually influenced words, pictures, and videos. Sure, that is all great. Good is always good. Good thoughts and good woods are great. But, they do not overcome the bad deeds these people have enacted. Only good deeds overcome bad deeds. What are these people doing to right what and whom they have wronged?

It is like the whole concept of karma. Some people falsely believe that if they do good then their bad will be balanced out. How can that even be possible? Just because you do good for some-thing or some-one else that does not undo any bad you did to a specific person!

I had one friend who when he was getting to the later days of his life totally turned to religion. He was one of those people who had screwed a lot of people over. But, he got rebaptized in his later years and he believed he was cleansed—that all his bad deeds had been erased. When he would tell me this I would just sit there in disbelief. How could he even believe that? He had hurt the lives of so many people but he thought simply by getting baptized he was free and clear? Wrong!

Do people deserve forgiveness? Maybe. But, only if they fix what they have broken. ...Only if they try and try and do and do until the damage they created to anyone's life is undone.

What If God Were One of Us?
23/Dec/2016 08:39 AM

To quote the lyrics and the intent of the Joan Osborne song, *"What if god were one of us,"* it was quite appropriately brought into focus yesterday when the President-Elect's daughter, Ivanka, her children, and her husband were verbally accosted in the main cabin (formerly called economy class) of a *Jet Blue* airplane yesterday. First of all, one has to question, why were her family and herself be flying on a commercial jet. I mean, both her and her husband are very-very rich, not to mention the wealth of her father our President-Elect. What was the purpose or the point? …To demonstrate that she was one of us? I don't know. Hell, I won't even fly in the main cabin of an airplane!

Then, there was the guy, who saw her and felt it was his right and necessity to accost her. Prior to that his husband/partner (I've heard him called both in the news) tweeted as to the oncomingness of the confrontation. This all goes to the point and the purpose of all of this and who do people (any of us) think we are—what gives us the right to go after anyone?

Many people believe they have the right to say anything to anyone they want. But, what gives them the right? I think back to a situation that occurred a number of years ago. A friend of mine worked at a supermarket in Redondo Beach. Then President Bill Clinton's brother used to live in the area. He looked a lot like the president. He was in the supermarket and a bag boy decided he had the right to insult the president and say to the brother someone should kill him. A few minutes later the Secret Service was in the store and the bag boy was arrested.

Just because you think you have the right to say something does not mean that you do! That is simply arrogance! You need to earn the right to do anything in this world. Without that your words mean nothing.

The President-Elect daughter's children were there on the plane with her. Apparently, the man had his child in his arms. Yet, he decided to spout negativity to Ivanka. Bringing children into any equitation where negativity is involved is simply wrong!

I think back to a time when I was going to McDonalds on Pacific Coast Highway a number of years ago. There was a car parked right in the driveway, pretty much blocking everybody who was trying to get in or out of the place. They were using the driveway as a parking space to eat their food. When I walked by I nicely mentioned this to them. The couple, with their two children in the backseat both totally went off, *"Fuck you, go fuck yourself, we'll do what we fucking want..."* I mean it was hardcore. Sure, there was a part of me that wanted to kick their ass (at least the male part of the team) but mostly I could not believe what they were doing to their kids in the car and that's all I expressed to them as I walked away. But, I am sure my words fell to deaf ears. Think what the life of those kids was like. Think about the kind of people they grew up to be experiencing that type of a negative, combative influence. It's scary... And, that's one of the main sourcepoints for how the world gets fucked up. ...People negatively influencing the life of their kids.

Whenever kids are involved you really need to care more about them than anything else—you especially need to tone down and control whatever it is you may be feeling.

Now, on the airplane, there was apparently Secret Service in tow. It is said they did nothing as the flight attendant kicked the guy and his kid off the plane. Again, this goes to the why of the situation. Why fly commercial when you have to have Secret Service with you—especially when you can afford so much more? And, why did the Secret Service immediately not intervene? One would think that they should have. ...That it was their job. The whys and the wherefores can be anyone's guess but the entire situation is

All-Wrong. When I first read about it I thought it was one of those fake news stores that have been so prevalent of late. But, it was not.

It is kind of like when Denzel Washington recently said, in that great voice he has, *"If you don't read the newspaper, you are uninformed. If you do read the newspaper you are misinformed."* Of course, only someone who is locked in a different age and does not care about life and the environment still reads the paper newspaper. But, the information presented in newspapers is out there but can it be believed?

Anyway, I saw the clip when the aforementioned couple and their kid got to SFO. Again, why did Jet Blue let this guy get on another flight? They should have banned him forever! But, they did not. Charlie from TMZ caught up to the guy but the guy said nothing and hid his face. If you are going to be so bold and verbally attack a woman then stand up for what you have done and explain it! If this guy or anyone else for that matter (i.e. you or me) thinks they deserve to have a voice and attack people with it, then explain what you have accomplished in life that gives you the right to have that voice and to use it. Simply because you exist or you think something about someone gives you no rights at all. You have to earn the right to do anything.

I don't know… This whole situation leaves me with more questions than answers.

I can say, that we live in a strange time of transition. Mostly, because of the internet, people have grown bold in what they believe they can express and how they believe they are right and thus everyone else must be wrong. But, just because you believe something does not make it right or wrong, it simply makes it what you believe. You may not like a politician but that does not give you the right to attack his daughter. For you always must ask yourself, why are you attacking anyone? Maybe it's because you don't like what they do or what they stand for. Okay, but that is just you—

what you believe and/or maybe what your small circle of friends believe. But, belief is just belief, it is not fact. How many times, as you have passed through life, have you changed your beliefs about a thing, a person, or a situation? If you hurt anyone in the process of expressing what you believe it is you who is at fault. There will be a price to pay. You will pay the price. That is just the way of the universe.

Thus, the wise person understands that what they believe is simply what they believe. They do not judge—they do not attempt to force their beliefs on anyone for they understand that a belief is just a belief and it may change.

Mostly, don't hurt people and never-never damage the lives of kids!

Why Do People Do What They Do?
21/Dec/2016 09:48 AM

Have you ever been in a life situation and you are watching it unfold where another person is doing something and you step back and cannot believe what is going on. You cannot help but question, *"Why is that person doing what they are doing?"*

These situations can be small or they can be large. They can only effect the person who is doing them or they can effect the larger whole. But, what that person is doing is something you would not do. Yet, there it is, being done...

People do all kinds of ridiculous things in life. They do things based upon any number of reasons. Mostly, they do them because they do not think about the consequences of their actions. Most people pass through life thinking of nothing more than nothing.

This style of mindless behavior leads to all kinds of ramifications in a person's life; anything from driving themselves into financial bankruptcy onto getting beat up or being arrested and the list goes on. What is the commonality of this equation is that the person acts but not does not think prior to performing their action(s).

Many people decide to set about doing bad things in their life. Though they never look deeply in the reason of why they are doing what they are doing, none-the-less, they do what they do. Many times they unleash their inner dissatisfaction and/or personal anger at their life onto others. They do this as a coping mechanism. They do this to take the focus of their inner-mind off of themselves in an attempt to make themselves feel better about who and what they are or are not. This is also the causation factor for why many people overspend. They are seeking a drug to remove themselves from their own internal pain. What they do, they do, and in many cases they hurt other people in the process as they also damage the overall standing of themselves in life. So, what they do hurts many—not only themselves.

On the other side of the issue there are people who believe they are doing the right thing; yet, that, *"Right thing,"* leads them down a road to disaster. I have personally known a man that was attempting to help a woman who was being assaulted by some guy and he literally lost one of his eyes because the assailant turned the focus onto the man and cut his eye and his face. The man's heart was in the right place—attempting to help the woman but he paid a very high price. Were his actions ever truly appreciated by the victim? That is hard to know. But, what did occur is that she went on with her life but his life, due to his choice to help her, was altered forever.

As you can see, what people do is motived by the mindset of the moment and where their heart is. If they are operating from a good place, bad things can happen to them just as readily as what occurs to the person who passes through life mindlessly.

The key factor in all this is, do you do what you do from a space of refined consciousness or do to you do it simply to do it—the world be damned; if someone else is hurt in the process, so be it. But, if you are hurt than all that occurs is again you find a new reason to turn the blame from yourself and reenter the space of unconscious actions attempting to find a cure for your ongoing inner turmoil.

You cannot control what other people do. You can tell them what you think they should do. But, whether they will listen to your logic is anyone's guess. Most people do not. They live from a space of mindless doing; they hurt, they damage, the do until they can do no more. What is the result? Damage. Damage to their life and damage to the life of others.

As you cannot control anyone else's life—at least not without using brute force, all you can do is do the best you can do and do it consciously.

Whatever you do, whether you do it unconsciously or consciously; whether it hurts others or it helps them creates the next set of available options in your life; from which, you must again choose what you will do.

Do your words, do your actions help? Do they set up a better life in front of you or do they hurt you and others?

Help or hurt; your choice. Living life consciously, making conscious decisions; your choice.

But, if you think before you do, the outcome will always be better.

Who Paid the Price?
20/Dec/2016 09:19 AM

There is always someone who pays the price.

Life is about action. Life should be about conscious action. But, most people do not understand this concept. The life of most people is completely driven by emotion.

From a philosophic standpoint these people are living at the lowest level of human consciousness because they are not even aware enough to understand that they are driven solely by emotion. They simply pass from birth to death in an emotional blur. This is why those who walk the spiritual path, no matter what that spiritual path may be, are focused upon controlling their thoughts and thus their emotions. They are taught precise techniques to do just that. From this, comes a mind of calm, peace, and inner knowledge. For, if you cannot control your emotions, if you do not even have the ability to see that you are driven by emotions, then your life will be lost to a never ending rollercoaster of random stimuli that not only shapes and controls your life but the life of all those you encounter.

Whatever you personally do in life, there is a price to pay for that action. Whatever you personally do that effects anyone else, there is a price to pay for that action. If you do not even ponder this, if you do not take it into consideration than that is the ideal depiction of your life. You are only thinking about yourself. There will be a price to pay.

At the root of all rising human conscious is the individual consciously taking control over their mind. What this means is that instead of simply allowing emotions and opinions to control you, you enter into a conscious space of deciding to control them. Instead of lashing out and reacting, you focus and choose how you behave. From this, not only comes a mind dominated by self-control, it unleashes a pattern of no-conflict in your life—no creation of further debts to pay. Thus, other people are not negatively affected by a thought processes based solely in the concept of you.

Some people react little to what is presented to them by the outside world. They know, acknowledge, and comment about what is going on but they seem to be in control of their reactions. Though this is a much better space to be living in than the individual who allows their emotions to rage outwards to the world, this is not a person who is actually in control of their mental state. It is simply that through their developed personality traits they encounter the world in a calmer manner. From this, yes, less outward casting of developed action is given birth to but at their root they are not a wholly spiritually dispassionate person. They are simply more quiet about expressing what is within.

Most people want the world to be the way they want the world to be. Most people feel they have a right to cast judgment and voice their opinions about anything and everything they encounter. But, where does that mindset come from? It arises from from the state of self believing that it knows more and/or is more than all others who are out there. But, do you truly know more? Is your opinion more valid than anyone else's? Does your opinion need to be heard? If you think so than you are an egotist. If you express this mindset to the world, then there will come a price you will be forced to pay for this decision.

This brings us to the point of why some people choose to spiritually refine their mind. They understand that all crisis is given birth to by the mind of one person unleashing their thoughts about the non-understood actions of others out to the world. All problems of this world being in the mind of one person. From this, that one person will pay the price. From this, all those who encounter that one person and congregate to their thoughts and actions will pay the price. This is why so many lives are lost to unhappiness and chaos—they are based upon paying the price for non-defined actions instigated by the thoughts of the egotist.

Life begins with thought. If you cannot consciously control your thoughts, then your thoughts are influenced not only by your own personal emotions but by the emotions of others. Thus, at the heart of all true spirituality is learning how to be in control of your thoughts.

At the most elemental level of personal control is deciding to take control over your thinking mind. Most people never progress to this level of consciousness. They never even think about it. They claim they don't need it, they do not care, or express the question of why should they or anyone else be forced to learn how to control their emotions and/or what they spout out to the world based upon these emotions. But, all of this is simply an excuse to the truth that one does not possess the mental advancement to actually be aware enough to understand that their emotions, their desires, their opinions are all motived by the lower self—that by expressing them they are only seeking other people to agree with them. They do this because they want the assurance that they, that their thoughts, actually mean something. That they, as a person, are something.

The fact is, if you have to go outside of yourself to gain this sense of self you are operating from a very insecure mindset. You are not operating from the whole. You are only operating from the lower levels of self. It is as this point that you must ask yourself, *"Are you willing to pay the price for all that you unleash by existing at this level of consciousness? Are you willing to pay the price for all of the lives you influence by operating from a position of ego?"*

Most people never even ponder this question. Most people don't care. They don't care until the bill comes due for their actions. Then, once again, all they do is turn to emotional outbursts and justify them through blame and denial. *"Why is this happening to me?"* But, the why is very clear to see.

You are responsible for what you think, how you think, and what ensues from the actions based upon what you do motivated by what and how you think.

You can be more. You can control what you do based upon how you think. You can realize that you emotionally reacting to the world and then telling the world what you think based upon your emotions does not have to set the course for your life in motion. Instead of being controlled by your thoughts and emotions you can learn to control them. You can take the time, gain the mental awareness, and free your mind from the randomness of emotions. The techniques are out there. They are easy to find.

Do you want to be more? If you do, then be silent—silence your mind. Take the time, learn how to do it and then, instead of paying a price for all you do to yourself, all you do to others, you can leave the world a better place by creating no bill to pay.

The more silent you are, the more you are.

Demons Among Us
20/Dec/2016 07:28 AM

There are demons that walk among us. People who pretend to be one thing but are completely the opposite. People who lie about who they and what they are to get what they want. People who have some form of mental illness and either hide it from the world or are too mentally ill to even realize the fact that they are flat out nuts. In each and all of these cases, the demons come into the life of someone else and completely destroy it. Caring not about who they are, what they are, or what they have done, they move through their entire lifetime doing nothing but damaging the lives of all those they encounter. There are demons among us.

In most case, it is only after our life has been damaged by one of these demons that we actually realize who and what they are. Initially, we only see the facade.

Most of us believe in people—we want to believe that people are good, kindhearted, and are doing good things while acting in a positive manner. This is where we are taken in by the demon. From believing in the goodness of people, demons find an open door.

In some cases, we can see the demons among us. Are you ever out in public and you see someone talking to themselves? This is the obvious, early stages of mental illness. Thus, they are on the road to demonhood. Some people are just nuts. They are yelling and screaming wherever they find themselves. Demon... But, then there are those who have the ability to hide who and what they truly are. They may do this through lying, they may do this through pretending. Whatever the guise, what they do is hide from the world what they have the potential of unleashing once one allows them into their life.

Sometimes, at a distance, we can hear a person yelling, screaming, and raging in anger. These people are controlled by their demons within. If we can hear them, we know to stay away from them. The problem is, most of these people are masters of deception; they lie and they hide who they are and what they do. They do this so most of the people they encounter do not know who they truly are until it is too late.

This is the same with people lost to the realms of distorted relationships. Some people perform very misdirected and unconscious acts within the realms of a relationship. Sometimes the other participant is a willing participant. Other times, they were simply indoctrinated into whatever levels of wrongness is taking place. Knowing nothing else, they do not question what is going on or why. Still others are lied to by these demonic personages. They are deceived into thinking the person is one thing when they are the complete opposite. This is where the true and absolute damage to a person's life can occur. They were lied to thus all levels of damnation may occur to them and they may have no way out. Thus, all hope and all life is lost.

At the root of the demons who walk among us is deception. They lie. Whether that lie is a conscious action attempting to gain what they want from other people or if it is simply a reaction; hoping to keep their demonic condition in the shadows, these lies have the potential to destroy lives. We can all say that this person should not have the ability to behave in their demonic manner. And, we can say that we hope we never encounter these type of people. But, they are everywhere. It is only through a very discerning eye and a developed understanding of what traits to look for that any of us can keep our lives free from being invaded by a demon.

Liar are everywhere; don't allow them in your life. People who hurt people are everywhere; don't allow them in your life. People who deceive other people about who and what they truly are, are everywhere; don't let them into your life.

Study anyone and everyone you meet—any person you encounter. Don't let a pretty face fool you. Don't let someone who you think is smart fool you. Don't let someone who you think will be the answer to your desires control you. Know everyone you encounter before you ever let them close enough to demonize your life.

Then Verses Now
19/Dec/2016 07:29 AM

I often find it very interesting when someone brings up facets of the counterculture that was then verses the now. People harken back to the 1960s and the 1970s (when counterculture was king) but they always get it wrong. Some young people actually fall in love with an era, of a time gone past, and believe they should have lived THEN. But, they did not. So, the THIS is all they have—though some do pretend to be living THEN. But, why?

Like, I always say, *"You had to be there or you weren't there."*

Certainly freedom, truth, getting in touch with yourself, interacting with the cosmos, and generalized spirituality was high on the minds of many people in the 1960s and the 1970s. I know that was the case for me. But, that was not everyone. Many simply followed the fashion trends of that era and moved along to the next trend once it came upon the horizon.

The fact is, life was different back then. There was a different mindset in place. For example, (then) you would see people hitchhiking with their backpacks all across the country. They were cool, they were accepted, they were, *"On the road."* Doing that, traveling like that was a highly admired life-placement. Now, anyone doing anything close to that is simply considered a bum.

Spiritual consciousness was everywhere. Commonly, you saw Western-born Asians, Caucasians, and African-American wearing the garb of whatever ever Eastern-based faith they followed. Me too… Now, all of that, all of that Eastern culture that impacted America (and other Western countries) is left to is the yoga classes where housewives hope to make themselves look better. All sense of true-spirituality is gone.

This time period (today) life is all different. The inner-presence of the people has changed.

Sometimes I see someone, who lived during that period, still attempting to pretend it is still going on. They may do this by how they dress or what they speak. But, it is gone. It will never return. And, this fine. Time moves on...

Recently, there has been several documentaries made about the spiritual teachers of the then. The majority of them, however, have either been made by fan-boys or those who wish to cast a shadow over what a specific teacher had taught and accomplished. Casting doubt is easy, especially onto a person exiting in an era gone-by. But, the people who makes these documentaries weren't there, they didn't personally experience the teachings—maybe they weren't even alive yet, so they possess no intrinsic understanding of what was actually taking place. Back then, we (many of us) were seeking spiritual emancipation and enlightenment. If you cannot understand that desire, you cannot understand the motivating factor for the why. Thus, all of these documentaries are simply conjecture made from either a positive or a negative point of view.

Again, in recent times, I have met people trying to emulate/redo what some of these teachers of that era taught. At best, however, all these people do is regurgitate words first spoken by others. These newbies have nothing new to say. Why, because they have no deep inner-experiences of the truth—they have no personal realization. And, that is what set the teachers of that era apart. They understood that first being a disciple—first being a longtime student, before they ever tried to become a teacher was essential to an emancipated enlightenment where they possessed the actual inner-knowledge to teach.

Post the 60s and the 70s, the 80s came a long. People started wearing Member's Only jackets and thinking about how much money they were making and what they could do with it. Everything changed. But, that is just life—

particularly in this modern age; fashions and what is considered important changes overnight.

In times gone past, in other eras, it would take centuries to change anything. Now, as first the industrial age and then the information age came upon us, life could change in the blink of an eye.

But, does a person needing a deeper sense of inner-self and inner-knowledge change? That depends... Some people don't care. They simply pass from birth to death chasing whatever it is they chase at whatever point in their life they find themselves until they are dead and gone. Then, there are some misguided people, thinking they have something to give other people, so they rise themselves to the pulpit. But, if you think you have something to give, if you tell anyone a lie to tell them what you think they should hear, all that is ego. These people always fail. And, this is what has given birth to all of the claims about falsity and deception brought about at the hands of these so-called teachers. From this, all who hear this, come to believe all teachers are like this. And, I suppose most are. Most, but not all...

But, beyond all that—beyond all the superficiality that is Out-There, there is the In-Here. The place where the quest for inner-knowledge and deeper understanding still remains. Most, never look to this place until they are at the door of death. Then, they wonder how and why? Others, however, spend their entire existence piecing the vail, finding inner-knowledge and they do this with no ego attached. They do it without ever exclaiming, *"I have something to give you."* They do it, simply because that is who they are.

So, to all those looking back, to all the documentarians, to all the followers, and to all the disbelievers, you are missing the point. Whatever era in time you find yourself in, the knowledge was never stronger back then than it is now. Knowledge is truth. But, the only true knowledge is that which arises from within. This is a knowledge that perhaps someone can point you in the direction of but can only be truly known by you.

There is no ONE enlightenment. There is no ONE pathway to the inner truth. There is only you if you decide to care enough to care and find out what is the secret of your life and of this universe. Once you find that put, you tell no one, because you can tell no one—because you know it is your knowledge, not theirs, just like you understand that any true teachers only possess his (or her) knowledge, not yours.

Divine truth is a singular subject.

Good Verse Bad. And, Which One Are You?
16/Dec/2016 01:54 PM

Sometimes good people do bad things. Sometimes bad people do good things. But, in the overall expanse of a person's life, these one-offs are the rarity. At the core of who a person is—their life is either bad or it is good.

Which one are you? And, are you honest enough with yourself to be able to tell the difference?

What is good and what is bad is a simple equation. Does what you say and what you do help people or does what you say or do hurt people? Some misdirected individuals attempt to measure this in a calculation. *"Well, I help more people that I hurt."* If what you are saying—if what you are doing hurts anyone, it is bad. There is no kinda-sorta-maybe in this equation. If someone/anyone is hurt what you are doing it is wrong.

Now, ask yourself, *"What is the consequence for hurting someone?"* And, are you willing to pay those consequences for doing what you do?

Hurting can be large or it can be small. But, think about when you were hurt by someone, I imagine it hurt. When you hurt, it hurts. If you have been hurt, you know how hurting feels, so why would you ever do it to anyone else?

Some people when they are hurt use that hurt as a motivating factor and an ideology to hurt others. *"I hurt so they should hurt."* Many do this without even thinking about why they are lashing out and hurting someone/anyone. They just do it. But, a life lived without thought is a lost life. It is a life dominated solely by emotion. From this comes a constant state of lack of peace. People have done to you so you are doing to people so people will again do to you. This is never a good state to be living within.

Think about it, what have you done good lately? What have you consciously done to make someone's life better? What were the results?

Think about it, what have you done that was bad lately? What have you done based upon negativity, anger, dissatisfaction, jealously, or rage of late? Having done anything based upon those levels of negativity is something that is bad. What were the results?

Sometimes, certain people, feel better when they do something bad. If they do feel enhanced, justified, or any sense of betterment based upon bad deeds any thinking person will say to them, *"That is wrong."* But, the individualized-mind of this type of person justifies all kinds of things that it does—finding logic, as misplaced as it may be, it says it is okay to do what is being done.

No matter what you say to an individual who is embracing this mindset, they will not hear you. That is the definition of an ultimately bad person—they are told what they are doing is bad and they do it anyway.

Sometimes good people do bad things, that is one the unfortunate conditions of life. We all make mistakes. But, what sets a good person apart from a bad person is that they live their life consciously and once they have made a mistake they do not remake the same mistake. Plus, they attempt to remedy any mistakes they may have made where a person or persons has been hurt. Do you?

Good or bad is who and what you choose to be. Being good takes much more effort than being bad. But, the rewards are far more substantial.

If you are bad, if you are saying and doing bad things, do you want to stop? If you do, that is a good thing. Then, do it! Stop it! Stop doing bad things! No excuses, no justifications, just stop! Once you have stopped, then go about undoing the bad you have done.

You want to be a good person? That is what it takes.

Good is always better than bad.

Have You Failed?
16/Dec/2016 07:53 AM

People are filled with denial and justifications for where they find themselves in life. People, due to their denials and justifications, also find various means to cope with these instigated mental states; i.e.: lying, misdirected anger, criticism, onto become lost in nicotine, drugs, and drink. All of these actions are a means to cope with the fact that they are not happy with where they find themselves in life. Where do you find yourself in life? Have you failed?

Your life is defined by you. It is defined by what you want, what you are willing to do to get it, and what price you are willing to pay to get it.

In life, some people do achieve what they desire. Most do not. At best, most people spend their life walking a path towards achieving their life desire. Some are happy in walking this path. They have a desired end goal and they work toward achieving it. They understand that each step they consciously take gets them closer to their desired end. Each step is an achievement in and of itself. If they never reach their ultimate goal they are content in the fact that they tried to get there.

On the other side of the coin is the person who believes that they should already be there. That they should be there before ever talking the step-by-step approach to get there. They believe that they are better and know more than the people who have already gotten there. But, as they are not there, they are angry at all those who are there, all who are working towards getting there, and everybody else; just because… Thus, all kinds of chaos is set in motion in their life and the lives or all those around them; created by their misplaced desire-fueled emotions.

Finally, there are those who seem to have it all; have everything that you dream of—they have it and then they either try to take their own life or succeed at it. With this, no one can understand why.

The fact is, all life is rooted in you. It is defined by you and what you expect and what you want from YOUR life. If you want nothing, you are free. But, very few people can exist at this advanced level of thought.

Those who grow up in a world of less are oftentimes more satisfied with achieving less. Those who have grown up in a world of more; want more.

As the technological edge of the world has progress and most people are exposed to the all and the everything of all the world's people, one sees the MORE that many people have achieved. Thus, they want that more. Do you? Are you satisfied to live with less than what you have wanted? Or, does all you do not have, viewed from a position of what you want, cause you to walk down a dark, negative road in life?

For those people who do embrace negativity, how often do they ask themselves, *"Is what I am doing, what I am saying, how I am behaving, actually leading me to what I truly want from life?"* Most of them do not have the mental aptitude to ponder this question. They simply react to the emotion of feeling what they are feeling, based upon all that they want to be in life, but are not.

What about you? Do you ever study your life? Have you succeeded or have you failed?

If you have succeeded, good for you! If you have not, at least not in the sense of the all that you hoped for in your life, can you be whole in yourself in the space you find yourself living within? Can you accept the reality of your reality and do good things, say good things, create good things from the space where you find yourself? Or, do you lash out with lies, uncontrolled emotions, misrepresentations of your self, negative words, actions, and deeds that harm the lives of others and the world around you? If you behave in this manner, let me answer the initial question posed in this discourse, *"Yes, you have failed."*

Like I Always Say, Let's See What You Can Do
15/Dec/2016 01:53 PM

I was talking to a buddy of mine at the *Rose Bowl Flea Market* last Sunday. He's a big fan of No-Budget Cinema and he alluded to the fact that I must be spending twenty or thirty-thousand dollars to make my films. I told him no, my top budget is three hundred dollars. He was a bit surprised, like most people are when they hear this, but he's a savvy guy who's been around so he immediately understood that I can produce films for that budget because I own my own equipment and do much of the stuff myself.

I must paraphrase here and state that some of the films I did earlier in my career and many of the ones I did in association with Donald G. Jackson had much higher budgets. They were shot on film and shooting on film is very expensive. This being said, we shot all of them as if we had no budget. We never paid for locations, never got permits, we just went out there and got it done.

Every now and then, as an actor, I've been called up to The Bigs by some great filmmaker: Brian De Palma, Robert Altman, James Cameron, and most recently Adam Sandler. Whenever I am on those sets it is just scary how much is going on… I mean, in my most recent experience in the Steven Brill, Adam Sandler film, *Sandy Wexler,* the vastest of the production was just dumfounding. They literally shut down Sunset Blvd., on the Sunset Strip, so they could film there; midday. I can't even imagine what it took to do that. When it was time for my lunch, they had a driver take me from my trailer at basecamp and drive me a mile or two over to the old Tower Records building where they were serving the food. Then, they had a driver take me back. I even had my own stand-in. A guy who was a younger better looking version of me. ☺ I mean, on every level, what it takes to get these productions accomplished is scary.

I think back to when I was in the Stallone film, *Stop or My Mom Will Shoot*. There was a scene in that film, shot on Hollywood Blvd., just off of Western, at night. (Just a couple of blocks from where I grew up). The scene had a large garbage truck, supposedly driven by Sly, crashing through the walls of the building—literally crashing through, into my character's supposed art gallery. As I have never been one of those actors to just sit around in my trailer doing nothing, I had been out there watching them set up for this shot. When the shot happened, Sly, his handler, another actor, and my self were the only ones up in loft above what was supposedly my character's gallery. Sly hadn't seen any of the set up for this shot so when the truck came crashing through the walls, he didn't expect it, and jumped back. Me, I had been out on the street and saw that the truck was chained down so it could only travel so far. Afterward he joking exclaimed to other people, *"That guy,"* (meaning me), *"Was scared but I was all good."* Sly, great guy. ☺

Now, that scene never made it into the final cut of the movie. Why, I don't know. I think maybe it would have helped. As the movie was kind of a flop, I doubt a director's cut or any DVD version, with the unused footage, will ever be released. But, that's Hollywood… And, this goes to the whole point of this—tons and tons of money is spent on these films. I don't think the average person can even fathom the over all goings on of what goes on.

Do I wish my film's had a bigger budget than three-hundred dollars? Sure. But, it is a little late in the game for me—I'm kinda old. So, I doubt I will ever be at that high-end level as a producer or director. But, that's okay…

After my part was done shooting on Sandy Wexler I thought to tell Adam or one of the producers, *"Hey, I've done some production work, maybe I could help out."* But, the level of productions I have worked would probably be way below their expectations. So, I never said anything. ☺

In any case, this all goes to you—you, the person out there... The wanna-be filmmaker and/or the critic. Like I have long said, and something that has been quoted many times, *"What is a film critic? With very few exceptions, (i.e. Bogdanovich), it is someone who doesn't have the talent or the dedication to actually make a movie."* But, you can make movies! You can get them done! They can even have some production value, even if you only have a budget of three-hundred dollars.

Throughout my career, either in writing or in filmmaking, I have been told so many times, *"You stuff is shit. I can do better."* But, not one time, in all of these years, has anyone who said this every went out there and wrote a book and got a publisher or actually made a movie that received distribution. It's easy to cast shade. It takes no effort. Creating is hard. That takes focus. That takes dedication.

Now, on the other side of the issue, there are a lot of people out there who have used my philosophy, adapted it to their own understanding of filmmaking, and made some fun films—even if they had no budget. But, like my aforementioned friend, there are fans out there of No Budget Cinema. So, it doesn't have to cost big money to get your project done. It doesn't have to cost big bank to get someone to watch it. Just shut up about other people and DO IT! Create something! Give your art to the world! You never know where it will lead.

100% Indian Hair
15/Dec/2016 08:26 AM

I was in the hood yesterday. As I was driving along I noticed a sign in the window of a beauty shop. You know, one of those signs that has the colored letters moving across the screen. It said, *"100% Indian Hair."*

For those of you who may not know, some African-Americans like to put hair extensions in their hair. ...The one's that have that long flowing black hair; that's what they have done. Apparently, from what I've been told, East Indian hair is the best.

Sure, some women want to make their hair and (I guess) themselves look better. I get it. But, what is the cost? Yeah, if you have money you can buy the hair and pay to have the extensions put in. But, think about the woman in India who had to have all of her beautiful hair cut off. A place/a country/a culture where, in many cases, a female is defined by her hair. Did they simply want to do it? No, they did it because they needed the money to survive.

Do people ever think of these things? Most do not. They simply see something they want and if they have the money they buy it with no thought of who paid the true-cost for them getting what they wanted.

India is poor country. I mean, in many places when you walk down the street, you feel like you are walking through the Armageddon apocalypse.

Many of these people are so poor that how they live and what they live on is indescribable. All some of these women have is their hair. That is their only commodity. That is all they have to sell. And, I am sure they are only paid a few cents for it. They are certainly not paid the several hundred dollars that I am sure it costs to buy it here in America.

Have you ever had to sell something you really cared about simply to survive? I have. If you haven't you are very lucky. Maybe, if you found yourself in times of financial need you could go to your family or something like that… But then, the fact is, you have never been tested. You have never had to put yourself, and what you care about, on the line simply to survive. These people in India have to live like that everyday. They do anything they can to survive—they sell anything they have to sell; i.e. their hair.

Most people, even if they are not wealthy, they make their way through life simply guided by what they want—going from one desire to the next. Ask yourself, do you ever think about what it costs someone else for you to get what you want? If you don't, you are a very selfish, very unconscious person. You should really be contemplating this with every thought of desire that comes to your mind.

Do the people who buy and then wear this, *"100% Indian Hair,"* ever think about where that hair came from—what is the life of the person who had to sell their hair actually like? Probably not. They simply think, *"I look good."* But, if you look good at the life-expense of another person you don't look good at all.

Think!

Drama, Melodrama, and Lingering Effects
14/Dec/2016 08:35 AM

With the ever-changing landscape of health insurance here in the States, I began going to a new doctor yesterday. As you may know, whenever you go to a new doctor they ask you questions about your previous medical history. *"Did you ever have any operations?"* I told him about the craniotomy I had after a girl ran into my motorcycle and nearly killed me when I was twenty-one. *"Did it leave you with any lingering effects?"* This made me smile. I wanted to scream, *"What do you think? It changed my entire life!"* But, my answer was, *"No, I guess I was lucky."*

All this set my mind to thinking back to the period of time that culminated with me being hit by that car. It was a very intense period. An intense period that left a lot of lingering effects in a lot of people's lives. I mean, many of us encounter those periods in our lives. In fact, no matter what the event, large or small, it can leave a lingering effect upon us.

How you encounter and react to those life-changing events is defined by how you set up your life prior to those occurrences and how you deal with them after the fact. Thus, it all comes down to choices; the choices you make and the choices other people involved in those event make. Ultimately, if you do not have any stability in your life; no safety net, the minute something tremendous occurs it can be devastating. It can take your whole life away. Thus, you should always think about what you are doing, why you are doing it, and what are the larger ramification of what you are doing.

Life… It is all based in the choices you make.

All this being said and since I mentioned it, let me tell the aforementioned story; a very abridged version of:

When I was sixteen, my main high school bud, that I have often referred to as Saturday Jim in my literature, introduced me to this guy, Mike, who had moved from Hollywood out to the valley the year before. Prior to that he lived in one of those junky Hollywood bungalow apartments with his father who was a weird little guy, looked a lot like Charlie Manson, and hung out with some of the seediest people: drug dealers, post Vietnam hitmen, ex-cons, you name it. Already a high school dropout, Mike's mother took him away from all that. In the valley he immediately met a girl with Asperger's, (a high functioning autism), and they got married the next month. His mother and her new African-American husband then rented them their very-nice three-bedroom house for only $100.00 a month. An insanely low rent. My bud, Saturday Jim quit school to work at a liquor store—a place where my sometimes buddy Charles Bukowski would frequent. (The first documentary ever done about Bukowski was done by PBS. I believe you can find it on YouTube. In that doc you can see Buk in that store). Anyway, each Friday night, after he got off of work, at about midnight, Saturday Jim would call me up, I would pick him up, (he didn't yet have a car), we would load up our guitars and amps, go over to Mike's, and we would party our brains out until Monday morning when I would show back up at Hollywood High School.

Mike's mother, eventually seeing what was going on, (as it wasn't just us partying there), kicked him and his wife out and they moved into a small single apartment a few blocks away. After high school, when I was about to start college and needed to get my own apartment, there was one available in his building. I moved in. This was one of those building full of all the drug takers, wanta-be musicians, and aging nobodies with no place left to go. My friend Mike and I played music there all the time.

As this was a building full of the young and the misdirected, all kinds of things went on. I met a girl. Though pretty, nice, and heartily walking the spiritual path, she had a very checkered past that did not leave her alone. I mean, very checkered. (A checkered past I couldn't get past). This checkered past was undoubtedly fueled by the lingering effects of a complicated childhood which lead her to making bad decisions. In any case, no matter what I would do, (and everything I did, I did very consciously), this girl would not leave me alone. She would show up with no place to live and me, being who I am, would let her live… Which lead to all kinds of complications.

Anyway… A new couple moved in. He, a musician. Though I never saw him play music. Mike and I would jam all the time; him never. His wife, however, the first night she was there, set her eyes on me. I could see it. I could feel it. She told him she wanted to go up to my apartment to play my Wurlitzer electric piano. She played me instead. All-good… The guy, her husband, began having an affair with the girl upstairs from their apartment who just had a baby. That girl's husband, a true bad ass, found out and kicked the shit out of all of them—deservedly so. During the chaos, I did something that I still feel bad about because children should have the right to choose even though they are only six or seven months old. The fighting raged on, the baby was screaming; to calm him down I gave him Shaktipat and initiated him with a mantra. He stopped crying. He smiled. But, one shouldn't do that. A couple of days after the incident, that new mother, her girlfriend and I went out; let's just say she didn't learn her lesson.

This all culminated with the whole young crew of the building deciding to move into a farmhouse in Tarzana. For those of you who may not know, the San Fernando Valley was once filled with farms and ranches. As the populous of L.A. grew, it was overtaken with settlement. But, some of the large properties still remain, even today. Anyway, they invited me to move in with them, but that was all too hippie commune for me and I could see what was to come. What was to come? The musician guy got pissed off and he took off with everyone's rent money. They were all evicted. His wife, who was initially only having an affair with me, decided to have sex with everybody. Then, they all had to move out. One guy ended up homeless. I saw him a few years later living on the streets. Most, I don't know. Mike, he had fallen for this one little teenage, hanger-on girl, and left his wife. He didn't drive so I drove him and his new girlfriend up to a one-room cabin in the mountains above Bakersfield where his fifty-something year old father was living with his thirteen-year-old girlfriend. Yes, thirteen… All of their worlds went to shit. All because of the choices they made, equaling lingering effects and some of them, I suspect, never really recovered.

A short time later, someone mindlessly smashed into my motorcycle and almost killed me. My life, never the same.

Lingering Effects… Yeah, I guess we all move on from what we experience, we move on to what is to come next. We move on to whatever degree…

I suppose I was the sanest, probably because I had my focus based in spirituality (though some may question my methods), on going to college, and in teaching the martial arts. But, in life, we all do what we do motivated by the lingering experiences of what went before. We have no choice. That is all we can do.

What do you do? How do you encounter life based upon what came before?

People Shouldn't Live Like This
13/Dec/2016 08:42 AM

Have you ever been in a really big city with millions and millions of people and you look around yourself and think, *"Where do all these people come from?"* I mean, whenever I am in Tokyo I often wonder, *"Where do all these people go at night?"* It just seems like there are too many people to actually have a place to go home to. I have lived there and I still wonder this.

In all big cities, be it Tokyo, Hong Kong, New York, Taipei, Mexico City, you name it, most of the people live in apartments. Meaning, they live in small spaces (sometimes very small) in vast buildings constructed to house them and keep them under control. But, just like the old saying goes, *"Too many rats in cage,"* this lifestyle gives birth unwanted interaction. ...You have to deal with your neighbors.

When I lived in New York, I had a loft in Chinatown. This was long before the rents went sky-high in the city. This was also long before the modern age of soundproofing. Though, due to the design of the space, I didn't have to listen to my neighbors, I did hear the constant noise of the city: day and night. It drove me nuts. Same with Hong Kong. The first time I stayed there for an extended period, no sleep. Too much noise of the city and my neighbors were constantly arguing in Cantonese. I hated it.

Living an apartment life it seems there often times comes problems with the neighbors. In New York, people are just rude. Tokyo, just the opposite. But, a neighbor is a neighbor is a neighbor. In an apartment you are forced to listen to them.

Most people who live in apartment's become acutely aware of their actions in relation to their neighbors while others are just rude, uncaring, and unthinking. But, you generally have very little choice in who will become your neighbor. If you get a bad one, believe me, your life is screwed.

Though much of the world has evolved into this state and status, this whole process is just unnatural. People need their space. People need their privacy. People need to not be thinking if their neighbor is hearing what they saying and/or doing. I mean, some people actually find pleasure in listening to their neighbors through the walls. That's just sick, Other, avoid it at all cost; they wear ear plugs. But, what all this does is to set a sense of paranoia into life. Living like this, one is forced to (unnaturally) think about others. From this, one is taken away from the ability to focus on the higher realms of their Self. They are taken away from them SELF. And, this is not good.

Maybe their neighbor is unconscious, noisy, and rude, and removes them from their meditation. Maybe due to their neighbor's noise, artistic endeavors are hampered. Maybe they are disturbed from reading an important book by their neighbor. Whatever the case, by the actions of their neighbor, a person is taken away from making themselves and this life a better place.

For those of you who have never lived in an apartment you have never encountered this. That is a good thing. You are lucky. Feel lucky! For once you have lived in an apartment, and once your life has been altered by your neighbor(s), you understand the too many rats in the cage syndrome. You realize your life/what you were supposed to be has been hampered at the hands of someone else for no other reason than too many people in one place and not enough money to be somewhere else. This is never a good realization to have.

In Tokyo, not far from *Yoyogi Station,* off the *Yamanote Line,* there is this one old-school Japanese house. An old guy lives there by himself. This house is surrounded by apartment buildings. How and why it was allowed to remain I do not know but I walk by in periodically and say,

"Hi," to the guy who is living there as he is commonly outside working on something. It is really beautiful. It is a true testament to culture. It is a space of wholeness, completeness in Tokyo's vast sea of apartment dwellers. If only all us city dwellers could be that free.

Second Hand Fame
13/Dec/2016 02:31 AM

It has always stuck me as curious how certain people climb on the coattails of the creative and find their way to fame via using the name, production, and/or the method created by someone else. In some cases, I believe this is a very conscious decision to bask in the glory, (whatever that glory may be), of what some other person has created. In other cases, it is actually to hurt a specific person by saying negative, untrue, self-serving, or straight out bad things. But, whatever the motivation may be, whether it be conscious or not, what occurs is that someone becomes noted for their association with a person or with a craft that they had nothing to do with creating simply by talking about it.

This has happened to me more than once. And, from a personal perspective, I cannot understand why the other person(s) would let something like that happen to themselves in the first place. For all they have done is to tie themselves to me throughout eternity. Sure, maybe they became a bit more famous because of it, but at what cost? All they have done is hitch themselves to my bandwagon and they have taken the ride for free. Do people not think that there is a karma associated with that? Not to be cruel but how young was Gene Siskel when he died and did you see what happened to Roger Ebert's face?

Now, I certainly understand that I am a small player in the grand scheme of things, so I find it very strange that this would happen to someone like me at all. But, I guess that is the cost one pays when you create something. People want a part of it—a part of it for free. They want it for free when they paid none of the life-dues that I had to pay to get to where I could create something in the first place.

Since I was a kid I have witnessed this—ever since the trash magazines were attached to the cash registers at all the supermarkets, they would say this and they would say that about whatever celebrity was a celebrity at the time. And, I guess they still create those mags, though more of the focus has shifted to the internet. Programs like TMZ have created an empire by doing this—making all of the talkers on the show famous in the own right—famous for talking about someone else and what someone else has created.

Certainly, there have been a few reviewers who have become very famous with their own newspaper review columns, radio and TV shows; simply for loving or hating what someone else created. But, what does loving or hating what someone else created actually mean? The reviewers didn't do anything—they went through none of the trials and the tribulations to get the project actualized, all they did was to love it or hate it. What does that even mean?

Some people are good at this. I guess they are highly motivated. They set out on a course and they make a name for themselves by talking about the creation(s) of others. But, who are these people, what are these people? And mostly, why do they get to be famous simply because they attach themselves to someone else? Why do they get to take a free ride on the fame, the notoriety, and the creative blood, sweat, and tears of another person? What have they personally conceived and created?

Again, from a personal perspective, those people who did this in association with me, did nothing for me. In fact, they hurt me way more than they helped. They never reached out a hand of friendship, they never asked if I needed any help on a movie, with a book, with anything… None of them have even met me. Yet, they believe they know me well enough to judge my work, my thoughts, my actions, or me. And, what do they get for doing it? Free fame.

Now, I am not talking about the people who get out there and actually do something with their life; whether that is making a movie, writing a poem or a book, playing some music, painting a painting, taking a photograph, kicking a kick, whatever... If anything I have said or done helps,

GREAT, take full advantage of it! Adapt it and make it your own. And/or, if you want to say something nice about me, *"Thank you!"* But, to latch yourself onto someone just to take a free ride, that is just wrong.

Now, I have referenced myself a lot here but that is really not the focus of this piece nor is it what I meant to do. But, you know, free-form thinking and all… It just kind of happened.

The point I am trying to make is, do what YOU do. Make your own art form. Or, as they used to say in the 60s and the 70s, *"Do your own thing."* Don't jump on someone else's bandwagon just to make yourself look like some kind of something. Do something/anything from your own source of inspiration and creativity. Do it yourself! Create it yourself! Talk about what you have created, not about what someone else has created. From this, the new/next art form may be given birth to. Don't tie yourself to and ride someone else's bandwagon to fame. That just makes you look like you have no personal inspiration to create something uniquely your own. Create YOU. I've already created me. Get off the bus and stop taking a free ride.

What You Give to Who(m)
12/Dec/2016 07:41 AM

I was speaking with a friend of mine yesterday and they were lamenting about how they had to buy Christmas gifts for all of their office mates of which there are about twenty. Now, if you think about this, even if you only spend five dollars on each person, that add ups to one-hundred dollars. But, most people don't want to look like they are giving out cheap gifts so it will probably cost a lot more. I jokingly chimed in and said I would go to the ninety-nine cent store for them and buy everyone sunglasses. That would only equal twenty dollars ...Everyone needs sunglass don't they? Of course, they said, *"No."* Then I suggested I would buy everyone a plate. You know, the kind that you eat off of... Think about it, we all can use a plate.

I guess I should explain something here, for those of you who are not familiar with the ninety-nine cent type of stores. They sell all kinds of weird and very useful stuff for only ninety-nine cents. Anyway...

All this got to me thinking about the whole process of giving during the holiday season and how many of us are forced into giving things to people we don't even really care about. Plus, we are forced into spending a lot of money in doing it. ...Money we may not have.

Now, as stated in the previous blog, giving is a good thing. But, there is a much more humanistic/spiritual element to giving than the one that is embraced during the holiday season. Here/now, many people are forced into the giving. ...Giving, *"Things,"* when maybe they can't even afford to do it.

Think about this, how many gifts have you received over the years that either you did not want, did not like, or can't even remember who gave them to you? Think about this, how many gifts have you given to other people that they didn't want, didn't like, or can't even remember that it was you who gave it to them? Think about this, how many gifts have you given to someone—to a person you cared about and then they threw them away or gave them away?

I learned this lesson the hard way, many-many years ago. I am sure I have told this story someone else before, but… Here it goes… When I was a teenager, freshly walking on the Spiritual Path, I had a good friend who was walking the path with me. Christmas came and me, finding my way on the Spiritual Path—believing all I had read and the like, I thought the best thing I could give him was my mala (prayer) beads that I wore and meditated with everyday. Though I truly loved them, I gave them to him. He was my spiritual friend; right? The next day I get a call from him and he tells me instead of cherishing them, he gave them away to someone he just met because that's what spirituality is, no attachments. Wow… I was devastated. Maybe what he said was true. But… The fact is, to this day, I have never found another set of prayer beads that I have been that connected to and/or cared that much about.

Here's the thing, most people don't care. They don't care about what you care about. They don't understand what you care about and/or why. Sure, there is all this pseudo spiritual mumbo jumbo about no-possessions, no-attachment, and all of that. But, this is life. This is reality. We all care about certain things. Maybe we shouldn't but we do.

In many case, during this holiday season, people also give more than they financially can or consciously should. They put themselves into debt and the people they have given to do not even care. Me too… In times gone past I have followed that path. Not good!

So, I can say, spend consciously during this season but many people will not. They will not go to the ninety-nine cent store.

It is like I think back several years to when someone gave my lady a bottle of Charles Shaw (no relation) wine for her office Christmas party. This wine is commonly known as, *"Two-Buck Chuck,"* as it only costs two dollars. It is sold by a chain of stores here in So. Cal. called Trader Joe's. Now, some people balked at this gift. But, for any of us who appreciate wine understand, the price of a bottle of wine has very little to do with how good it tastes. And sure, it is not the most highly refined wine but, Two-Buck Chuck tastes pretty good! What more can you ask for in a gift than that?

Which brings us back to the main premise of this discussion, a plate from the ninety-nine cent store... Think about it, don't you use a plate everyday? I mean, how totally useful if that? If someone would give me a plate I would totally appreciate it and say, *"Thank you."* I mean sure, what I really want is a Gibson L5-S, (I should never have given mine away), but I doubt anyone cares enough about me to buy me one of those... So, a plate from the ninety-nine cent store, All-Good. ☺

You should really appreciate the gifts people give you. You should really think about the gifts you give other people—whether you are forced into it like my friend or not. Caring and giving is not based upon what it costs, but what it means to you, what it actually can do for the life of the other person, and how it effects both of your lives.

Using Your Power for Something Good
11/Dec/2016 07:14 AM

As we are barreling our way down the road to Christmas and everyone is thinking about what they are going to buy for somebody, I think this is an ideal time for everyone to take a look at the big picture and ask themselves, *"What I am doing to make someone's life better?"*

Most people become very lost in the concept of, *"I."* They only think about themselves, what they want, and who they want it from. This is where the whole concept of the Christmas list came into play. Though this season should certainly be a time for giving, in many cases most people see it as a time for getting. Thus, they make a list of all that they want and they pass it out to the world. *"Here, give me this."*

Sure, people buy friends, family, and co-workers gifts. Why? For the most part this is because they have to. There may even be that someone you really care about that you want to give that something special too… But, everyone else, it becomes simply a job.

But, let's go beyond all of this. What are you giving back to the greater whole? Are you giving anything to anyone that you do not personally know and are not forced to give to? In fact, ask yourself, do you ever spend any time actually thinking about what you can give to someone, anyone, everyone that will make their world better? If you don't that is very sad.

Everyday that I wake up I have a plan for what I can do for someone or something. Be it large or small I want to give back every single day.

I truly-truly think that everyone should be doing this. Think how much better the world would be if people actually cared enough to stop only thinking about themselves and started thinking about the all, the everything, and the everyone.

Why do you only give gifts to people you know? Why can't you give to people you don't know? This is the Christmas season, why can't you care enough to care and get out there and give?

Really… Try it. It will make you a better person and the world a better place.

No Bill to Pay
10/Dec/2016 08:12 AM

    The other night this one relatively famous actor got arrested for smacking his Uber driver in the head. That was a good thing. So many people in positions of power think that they can do anything that they want, behave in any manner that they want, and get away with it. Many average people in life behave in this manner, as well.

    Have you ever had a criminal court case hanging over your head? Have you ever been sued by somebody and you are constantly thinking about the cost of your lawyer and wondering what will be the outcome? If not, that is a good thing. But, a lot of people get away with a lot of stuff that hurts other people and they just do not care—they pay no price. What if the actor was not called out on his bad deed? Then, he would have gone on living his blessed life, feeling all empowered and not even thinking about the life of the person that he damaged. Do you say or do things that hurt other people? Do you then have to pay the bill? Or, do you walk away scot-free?

    So many people do so many bad, illegal, immoral things and they get away with it. I mean, these things go from physically hurting a person, stealing from them, onto slandering them on the internet, or downloading copyright protected content such as music or movies from offshore sites or file sharing websites for free. All of these things: large or small are wrong but people do them all the time. They do them and they think there is no bill to pay.

    From a personal perspective, I had this one guy just rip on me, telling untrue, misplaced falsehoods and lies about me; claiming I am some sort of a bad guy and then contact me telling me that he had only seen my movies via illegal online downloads and he wanted to review my movies so could I send him free copies so (I guess) he could rip on me some more. So, this guy not only diminished my income by watching my movies from some illegal site but he wanted to fuck me over further by talking shit about them once I gave them to him for free. No lie. That actually happened. I mean come on! Do people ever think about the wide-spanning ramifications of their actions?

Now, life and the misguided way some people behave amuses me no end. Hell, it equals blogs like this. ☺ But, being on the creative side of the picture I also see the downside—how internet bashing and internet stealing truly effects the life of the creative (like me and maybe you).

I have also know many people who have been hurt by physical and/or psychological violence. …Hurt by someone who did and does not care. And, this goes to the point of this blog… Many people do whatever it is they do without thinking about the impact of their actions and without caring about the repercussions of their actions. Do you? Or maybe, in some cases, they actually want to hurt a specific person. But, why does any person want to hurt in anyone? What is the benefit? What is the reward? And, more than that, what is the karma—what is the price of the bill you will have to pay?

I believe that most of us do care. We don't do things that intentionally will hurt anyone. If we do hurt someone, we own our actions, and we try to repair them. But, we all can fall prey to the allure of something free and some even find a way to quench their thirst for lack of self-esteem by doing things anonymously and intentionally to hurt someone else. But, ask yourself, those of you who partake of this type of action, what if it was happening to you—what if it was happening to someone you love?

Again, this brings us back to the why, the wherefore, and the ramifications of said actions… Long ago, I had lost faith in karma. But then, I started to see it in action. I have known people that literally rose to the top of the game in the film industry. They were living at the top of the world. But, they got there by screwing everybody they ever encountered over. But, then they fell. Karma got *'em.* They ended up just like the rest of us; doing the nine-to-five. I never wished this on them, but it did happen. Bad actions, bad choices, bad deeds equaled them living a bad life. Do you ever think about where the actions you are unleashing will lead the life you are living?

But, like I always say, even if a person does receive their karma for doing bad things to people, that does not give back what was taken from the person whose life they damaged.

So, this all comes down to the question(s), who are you? What do you do? How do you do it? And, why do you do? Can you be moral enough to not do it if what you are doing is wrong?

Growing up where and how I did I often saw how the juvenile delinquents would egg each other on. With a group mind one could be convinced that what they knew to be wrong was not. How much of your life do you live like that? How much of your life is guided by the negative words, the negative actions, and the negative guidance of others? How much of the actions of your life do you justify in your own mind? Or, do you just not care? Do you simply cast it to what you do is what you do, what you say is what say, and the world be damned?

This, here, is where we find the essence of how all things are born into this world. If you care you care. If you turn off your ego, turn off your power-tripping, turn off all of the damage that you may have encountered and actually try to do the right, the moral, and the good thing, then there is no bill to pay for your actions. With no bills to pay, the world becomes a better place.

Who are you? What do you take from the world? What do you give to the world?

Who Is Thinking About You?
09/Dec/2016 10:21 AM

Right now, take a moment and answer this question, *"Who is thinking about you?"*
Yes, you know who you are thinking about. But, who is thinking about you?

Now, ponder this... Why are they thinking about you? Is it something you said, something you did, or something that someone else stated that you said or did?

What is the implications of them thinking about you? What has their thinking about you done for and to your life? Has them thinking about you equaled something positive or something negative in your life?

Do you think about them, thinking about you?

Did you make them think about you?

Should someone be thinking about you but they are not? Are you thinking about them not thinking about you?

Do you wish someone would stop thinking about you?

Life is a complex process of human interactions. We meet or we hear about, then we think about. But, is what we are thinking about a person the truth about that person or is it simply something we or someone else has believed? When people think about you how much of what they think about is based in reality?

Has someone told a lie about you so people believe some untruth when they think about you?

We hear about people. We are told about people. What is based in truth and what is based in fiction?

We meet people. Is what they are saying the truth or is it a lie?

We meet people. Is what they are presenting to the world who they truly are or is it a concocted personification of who they want the world to believe them to be?

What do you say, what do you project to the world? How does that affect how others think about you? Is it the truth or is it a lie? Are you a fact changer? Are you a liar? And, how does that effect what people think about you? What will be the long term effect of people not knowing the true-truth about you? What is the truth?

When you think about people, what do you think? Does the thought of them make you happy, sad, intoxicated, or angry? Why do you think about people at all?

When people are thinking about you what emotions come to their mind? And, why?

Is someone thinking about you? Why are they thinking about you?

Sins of the Past
09/Dec/2016 09:36 AM

How much of what you said, what you did a day ago, a week ago, a year ago, a decade ago do you wish you could undo? Is there anything?

Most of us have done certain things in our life that we wish we could undo. A good thing to do is to right now take a look at your life—define in your mind what are those things that you wish you could undo. Now, ask yourself this, *"Why do I wish I could undo them—why do I wish they never happened?"* What is your answer? Is the answer that you wish you had not done them because they hurt someone else? Or, is the answer that you wish you did not do them because they hurt you?

Life is defined by the interactions we have with other people. How do you interact with other people? Do you think about you first or do you think about them first? Your answer to this will provide you with very deep insight into how and why you interact with life and with people in a specific manner. It will also provide you with insight into why it is that you do things that you later wish could be undone.

Truthfully, some people do not care. They do not care if they have hurt the life of other people so they do not look back to their past with any thought about anything that they wish they could undo. This is obviously a very selfish mindset. But, think about the people you have known throughout your life; have you ever met a person like this? Are you like this?

Some people also feel that they have the right to do and say whatever it is the want and they do not care about the effect they have on anyone else. In fact, they never even think about the effect of what they are doing may be having on someone else. This is where all of the problems of the world begin, the selfish mind.

In fact, some people actually want to hurt other people. Maybe they have been hurt or maybe they are just arrogant and self-involved. But, from hurting they somehow grow a deeper sense of self. But, saying or doing anything that hurts anyone only leads to further confrontation and the damaging of additional lives. Who are you? What do you do? And, why?

Most people do not think about others, at least initially, when they do what they do. They only think about themselves and this is what gives birth to situation creation where regret is born.

The thing is, at least if a person has regret about some of the things that they have done in their life this means that they have a conscience; it means that on some level they care about other people. Though most people may have only cared about themselves initially, once they realized that they have hurt someone else, they rethink their actions and have regrets.

Now, let's think about this… Of all the things you have done in your past that you wish you would not have done, how many of them have you tried to undo? Have you ever cared about the other person or persons involved in that action enough that you actually set about on course to fix that situation—whatever that situation may have been? Have you ever apologized? Have you ever put your own desires, your own ego, and your own perception of how you want to be viewed by the world on hold long enough to actual cancel out and remove from history what you did? Or, did you simply gloss over it, not truly caring about the other person, and provide yourself with a new set of self-motivated justifications while relishing in the assurances of your family and friends that it is only, *"Poor you,"* who has been slighted by the world?

I believe in life, most people are good people, most people are caring people, most people are nice. But, there are some that, due to whatever psychological programming they have instigated or have encountered in life, embrace only their lower self and they never step beyond the actions they have unleashed. Instead, they simply deny them, hide from them, and/or attempt to make them seems okay when they are not. Who are you? What do you do when you see that what you have done has hurt someone else? Do you care?

Life is a pathway. Life is process of growth. We all do what we do and in some cases we end up realizing that we shouldn't have done some specific something. But generally, one only realizes this when the care enough about other people to care about whom they may have hurt. Do you think about others? Do you care what you have done to their life? Do you take pride in damage? Or, do you feel regret about those you have hurt?

What ultimately makes you a good or a bad person is what you do when you realize that you have hurt someone else—what you do when you realize that your actions may have hurt you. Can you forgive yourself? Can you forgive the other person? Can you step up and actually be nice—be good—be better and undo what you have done? Or, is all that you do is lie and deny and hide from the actions you have instigated?

Life is about you. Life is about what you do. Life is about what you do to others.

What do you do? And, do you care what you have done? What are you doing today that you may regret tomorrow?

Is Your Life Empty?
Consciously Empty or Unconsciously Empty?
09/Dec/2016 07:51 AM

On the path of consciousness, we teach the individual to empty their mind—consciously empty their mind.

On the path of unconsciousness, (unconsciously living), people empty their mind through drink, through drugs, through various endeavors that distract them from what is really going on in their life—ultimately keeping them from knowing who they truly are and why they behave the way they behave.

What is the difference?

On the path of consciousness, you consciously empty your mind through meditation. Why? Because when you are consciously thinking of nothing, deeper inner-revelations are presented to you about your self and your interaction with your life and the universe—universal truths are exposed that you can never find by thinking about them.

Many people believe that they cannot silence their mind. In fact, many people who attempt to meditate find it impossible to stop thinking. Though forcing yourself to stop thinking, even if it is only for a few seconds, can not only provide you with insight into what non-thinking can reveal, it can also cause you much mental discomfort because you may feel that you are not strong willed enough to have self-control.

Drinking is easy. You simply drink something. Drugs are easy, you simply take something. Denial is easy, you simply deny all your faults and make excuses for all of your shortcomings. But, none of this leads to a deeper understanding of anything: no self-control, no self-discipline, no enlightenment; nothing… And, not the conscious kind of nothing.

Most people don't care. They want to be more in terms of the ways of the world: more money, more power, more beauty, more fame. They run from the fact that all that stuff is temporary. Disassociated from a deeper understanding of life, they care only about how they feel and about the what is out there that they want. But, ask yourself, has the pursuit of THAT, has the pursuit of all that unconscious nothing, answered all of your dreams? Yes, you may have passed from then to now, but can you say, right here, right now, that you are fulfilled? If you are, good for you. End of story… Fade out. But, if you are not, then maybe it is time to try something else—try viewing life is a different manner.

First of all, to meditate, you do not have to sit cross-legged on the floor. Any THING can be your meditation as long as it takes your mind away from THAT and brings it to a state of silence: running, biking, dancing, walking, or sitting cross-legged on the floor. Any place you can find silence and embrace the conscious emptiness is the space of meditation.

What you do is not all that important. How you do it, however, is. How you focus your mind while you are doing IT is what makes anything a meditation as opposed to simply a physical activity.

For example, yes biking can be a good form of physical exercise. But, as you bike, are you thinking about getting from point A to point B and what you will experience once you arrive. Or, can you allow your mind to merge with the action, think about nothing else but the purity of the space of consciousness you're living and from that enter the space of no-mind.

In the martial arts, many physical techniques give birth to the meditative mind. They are developed to do so. Everything from meditatively drawing the sword onto the physical forms, most commonly known as kata, allow the martial artists to enter into a state of no-mind. Though one is doing, they transcend the doing and become one with the action. This same understanding can be applied to all that you do. It is simply you who must decide to activate this level of mental interactive conditioning in your thinking mind and move it towards the meditative mind.

Thought is a condition of life. No-Thought is a choice. Those who choose the ladder find a new level of personal understand and universal awareness that is not known by the vast majority of the world population.

Who are you? Do you believe your thoughts are all that important that you cannot/should not turn them off for a moment?

Silence is golden. Quiet your mind, you will be amazed what you will find.

Have You Ever Broken Something?
08/Dec/2016 09:54 AM

Have you ever broken something either by accident and intentionally? Once it was broken, did you care enough to try and fix it? Once it was broken, if you did care enough to try and fix it; when you did repair it, was it ever truly the same?

Breaking is easy. It takes very little effort. All you have to do is do it. But, once it is broken, then what?

Do you ever think about the implications of what you break before you break it?

Let's take a moment here and think about this... Say you have a cup and in moment of rage you throw it and break it on the ground. No big deal; right? Or is it? How much did that cup cost you? What did you have to do to earn the money to buy that cup? What about the person who made it? What did they have to go through, in their life, to actual create something that you mindlessly broke?

Few people ever think about these things. In fact, they are so unthinking, they just do. But, *"Doing,"* without thought is one of the worst things you can do in life.

Say you broke something... Maybe you did it in a rage; maybe you did it by accident—do you ever try to fix it or are you so self-involved that you do not even care? This is a defining factor for life and what becomes of a person's life. For how you do what you do and how you react to all that you have done is what sets the course for your life and what will come next in your life into motion.

I think back to when I was three or four years old. My father got mad at me about something and he took my stick horse and broke it over his knee. I was devastated. I loved that stick horse.

Now, I suppose I should preface this section by stating I grew up in a very different period of human history then is taking place now. Parents generally disciplined their children very harshly. In the world of today a lot of what took place would be called, *"Child abuse."* But, everyone I knew got the belt when their parents thought they did something wrong. I guess that is why so many people of my generation grew up to be so abusive and psychologically misaligned. Not good but this is part and parcel for the causation factor of the truth. And, a motivating factor for what goes into the process of breaking in the first place.

Which takes us to the point of this discussion again; breaking… Once my father had calmed down, he glued and taped by stick horse back together. He told me it was a saddle. I thanked him, but it was never the same. Every time I looked at it all I could remember was his breaking it and how it was now nothing more than a broken object that I once loved so much.

See how easy it is to break things… See how impossible it is to put things back together…

Now, I am not asking for a, *"Boo hoo,"* moment here. This is just life and we all go through what we go through. But, what this is, is a time to think about yourself and what you are doing in and with your life. Think about when something was broken that you loved. Yes, maybe you were very enlightened about it and you let go of your attachment to it. But, was that simply because you really didn't care about it that much? Because I believe that if you did really care about it, the fact that it was now broken would really hurt.

This also goes to the fact of how and why some people relentlessly break the things of others. They don't care! It's not theirs! They do not care about the object, they don't care about the person, and in some cases they want to hurt the person by breaking something they care about. How fucked up is that? But, think about how many people behave in this manner. Do you?

Life is broken in many ways. It is not solely objects that are broken but actions taken by others people that can truly break another person's life. It can cause people to become ill. It can even instigate someone beating or killing another person. Or, make a person kill themselves.

If you are so vain that you do not care about the breakage that you are unleashing I can tell you that you should be ashamed of yourself but I am sure that statement would fall to deaf ears. What I will say is, if you are intentionally breaking anything either through uncontrolled emotions or via direct intent, the next time something is broken in your life; something that you really cared about, that is the time to ask yourself what have you broken in other people's lives and how much time have you spent attempting to glue it back together. It may never be the same, but if you do not try then all you will ever be is someone who does nothing more than take things away from life and cast them to the realm of the broken. Which makes you what? Part of the broken. If this is you, what do you expect your life to become?

You can be more!

Higher Self, Lower Self and Which One Are You Embracing?
08/Dec/2016 07:49 AM

If you ask the average person what they think about the concept of Higher Self, they will more than likely tell you that it is a bunch of mumbo jumbo. …That all they care about is getting what and who they want in life and getting over on all those that they judge to be less than themselves. I get it… Most people are very preoccupied with whatever momentary reality they are living. If all is gong well with their life and they are getting everything that they want and no one getting in their way and stopping them from saying and doing whatever it is they want, all is well with the world. But, the moment this is not the case—the moment a person runs up against obstacles, they lash out and here is where the Lower Self comes into play. …They say and do hurtful, mean spirited, self-serving things. They do this to react to their desire, (whatever that desire may be), not being met.

The fact is, people are emotionally driven creatures. They want what they want and they want it now. If they don't get it or it is taken away from them; look out. The bigger they are; the more chaos they create when they are not getting their own way.

But, there can be a better way to live your life. Some call it, embracing the Higher Self. It is at this level each person, instead of simply reacting to life events, takes the time to study them, learn from them, and not be controlled by them. From this, negative karma is not born from the actions that are spread outwards by the person embracing their Lower, (Emotionally Driven), Self.

In the Eastern Tradition of Spirituality, the zealot is taught to enact, *"The Witness."* The Witness is you stepping back from whatever momentary, emotion driven, momentariness you are encountering and studying it as if you were another person watching you live your life.

Why should you do this? Because it gives you perspective. It allows you to step beyond the controlling hands of your emotions, look at all sides of the issue, see where it arose, how you may have caused it, what you did once it occurred, and how you are reacting to it in the here and the now. From this, a profound sense of Self Understanding is born.

It must be stated that enacting The Witness is far different from you being out of control of your mind and your mind taking control over you. Meaning, a similar occurrence of you being separated from your body and watching yourself from afar occurs in various forms of mental illness. It also may occur when you take hallucinogenic drugs. But, that is another subject altogether. Instead, enacting The Witness is a very conscious process that causes you to study you. It does not mean that you are being controlled by some out of control you. It is you very consciously watching you.

You should take a moment right now and try it. Simply STOP right here, right now. Close your eyes and see who you are, what you are, what you are feeling. Now look deeper, examine why you are feeling what you are feeling and perhaps even how you became you. ...What led you to the experience of you being who you are. Watch yourself. Who are you? What are you? Why are you? Watch the Self of you being you.

Most people never take the time to think about who they truly are, what they truly are, why they are doing what they are doing, and what led them to this place in life. They simply live. They simply react. From this, they go from one emotion or desire driven experience to the next. The love, they hate, they relish, they hurt. They do this without ever taken the time to understand why they are doing or feeling anything. Quite simply, this is call living a life driven by the Lower Self. Most people pass through their entire existence with our ever thinking twice about how they are truly living and how they are truly encountering life. Do you? Mostly, they never come to understand who they truly are.

So again; right here, right now, witness yourself. If you are taking the time to read this, you are probably not terribly emotional. This is a good time. When you are calm that is a good time to begin this process because it gives you a moment to slowly embrace this understanding and to begin to gain insight into how beneficial it is. For when you are emotional it is so much harder to evoke this practice. That's why you need to develop your sense of the Higher Self when there is none of your Lower Self in play.

Be More!

How You See What You See
07/Dec/2016 07:52 AM

Everybody enters each new life experiences with a preconceived notion about what they expect that experience to be. Some people are more open to allowing each life experience to be what each life experience is. Others, however… They want everything to be exactly the way they want it to be.

How do you behave?

Who do your think is the better person?

Some people shelter their life from ever encountering anything new. Others do all they can to constantly be involved with the new and the different. Who is the better person?

People who do not have a developed sense of self-awareness want to control everything. They want to be the one in control. …In control, they believe they hold the power. At least they think that they do.

This gives birth to the person who is very judgmental. We have all met people like this. First of all, they want to try nothing new and they do all that they can to keep themselves and everyone around them from encountering new life experiences. They often do this by being grumpy, demeaning, condescending, judgmental, and even angry. If they are forced to experience something new, all they do is completely remind all those around them how miserable of an experience they are having and how, if anyone else is receiving enjoyment, they should not be. Most of us do not enjoy interacting with a person who embraces this mindset.

Judgment comes from desiring an end result. But, judgment limits all possibilities of understanding new forms of thought.

Yes, we all enter each life situation with a framework of understanding that we have gained from previous life experiences. But, those with an open mind have the ability to enter new realms of understanding and gain new levels of refined wisdom through each new life experience.

There are those who are constantly looking for all that is new and/or different. Does this make them a better person? Not necessarily... Just as the person who enters all new life experiences with their mind already made up, the seeker can become addicted to the seeking. ...It doesn't matter what it is, as long as it is new and different. This frame of mind can move throughout all elements of their life, from what they do to whom they do it with.

It is important note, as I have long said, each life experience is defined solely by the individual; *"If you love hell it becomes heaven."* Some people enjoy very aberrant things. You most likely will not. Therefore, this discussion does not mean that you are expected to like what you don't like. It simply means that if you can free yourself from preconceived judgment you can enter into all things, *"Life,"* with the ability to truly see each thing for what it is and then determine, from the space of an open mind, if it fits into your overall life.

How many times have you tried something you thought you would not like and actually became quite surprised that you liked it a lot?

Some people falsely believe that judgment make them a more powerful person. Judgment does not. Judgment only makes a person look foolish. Especially if that person releases their judgment(s) to the world.

The essential element to living a self-actualized life is to be open enough to experience life; you may like something, you may not, that is simply the defining factor of personality. But, always be open enough to understand that you cannot truly know until you try and once you have tried, even if you do not like it, be whole enough onto yourself that you understand that other people do.

To All That In The No That
06/Dec/2016 02:11 PM

"Did I wake you up? Oh good, what are you doing? Can you meet me over at McDonalds? I am so bored!"

I heard this conversation today when I was in a thrift shop looking for some wardrobe for my next Zen Film.

How can you be bored in this life? I just don't get it. There is so much going on. There is so much to do. Everybody today can be an internet author, a poet, a newshound, or even with the phone the guy was holding in his hand, a photographer or a filmmaker. It is all out there and it is all free. How can you be bored?

In life, it is obvious, we all seek something to do—we wall want interaction. But, look around you, there are a million people out there. You can interact with any one of them—all you have to do is go up and say, *"Hi."* From there, who knows what world of magic will be born.

Some people are locked into the realms of the nine-to-five. They have their job to do. That is a good thing. They are taking responsibility for their life while feeding and giving back to the economy of their society. Some people are not like that, however. Maybe they are on the dole, maybe their life is being financed by their parents, maybe they are retired, and from this they are locked into a world of not having to forge out a living so they become, *"Bored."* But boredom is created by your own choices within the life that has been given to you.

Boredom is a choice. It is how you encounter your life.

I think to this one homeless guy I have seen around for over a decade. He has long grey hair and a long grey beard. He is always in the same location, just off of this main thoroughfare. When I would see him in years gone past, he used to be laying on this AstroTurf lawn that separated this gas station from the sidewalk. I guess the owners of the gas station didn't like him laying around on their AstroTurf all day, everyday, so they paved over it. The guy then moved to the bus bench right in front of this previous location. I guess the city didn't like him laying there so they removed the bus bench. Now, the gas station has put up these big boulders where the man used to lay. But, I drive by and he is still there. No AstroTurf, no bench, so he literally lays across these big boulders. I cannot even imagine how uncomfortable that is. But, he is there.

In India, he would be a sadhu. I mean I have studied with men who have spent *years-upon-years* never leaving their cave. They are considered saints. But here, in the States, no saints, just bums. But, there this guy is… Is he bored? Obviously not. He has a purpose, a mission. …Even if that mission is only in his own mind.

Most of us, when we are alone, seek mental stimulation. We read, we watch TV, we go on the internet. But, more than simply absorbing something Out There, the internet provides you with so much more. You can interact, you can create. There are great things to learn and to do on the world wide web. Certainly, there is the lowest level of human interaction that goes on upon the web, as well: insulting and trolling, the spreading of negativity and/or hate-speak. But, that is only done by those of low mind— those that hate themselves so they find someone or something else to take the focus off of themselves. They are out there; but just like the rude, the inconsiderate, or the bad people who walk the streets they can and should be ignored, avoided, and shunned. We can and should only embrace the positive for that is where all of the great things of life are created be they relationships, art, philosophic progress, you name it…

So, here we are: you and me. Here we are dong the, *"That."* We are living, we are learning, we are creating. There they are, those lost in the *"No-That,"* the nothing. Boarded, because they refuse to see that there is a world of beauty to witness, embrace, interact with, and create due to all of the inspirations that are out there.

So, whether you are creating poetry, literature, art, learning, living, or simply watching life pass by while laying on an uncomfortable boulder on the side of a busy street, there is always something to do in your life. By being part of the positive growth of this place we call, *"Life,"* you should never be board.

What About the Metaphysics?
05/Dec/2016 03:20 PM

I am often questioned why do I so rarely discuss the metaphysical realms of reality. Instead, I talk about psychology instead of parapsychology. The answer is fairly simply, this is reality.

The fact is, I actually have a Doctorate that I earned in the field of metaphysics back in 1985. Though the university was not accredited, it was a fully functioning university. Back then, it seemed that alternative forms of education were to become the norm. And, to a certain degree I suppose they did. But, people have become so judgmental and critical about anything that they do not personally believe in, thus and as such, I generally forgo mentioning that degree.

And perhaps, this brings us to the whole point of this conversation… Metaphysics is based upon conjecture, speculation, and unsubstantiated personally motivated understandings. There is all that Out-There. There is all this stuff that people wonder about, talk about, write books about, and charge people money for—telling them they are a conduit of whatever this or that element of cosmic energy but none of it is based in the here and the now of reality. It is based upon what a person believes. Sure, there have been tons of books written about all kinds of cosmic subjects, there have been movies made, both scary and otherwise, where these fictions are presented as fact, there have been people since the dawn of rising human consciousness that have promised a pathway to the great beyond but what has actually changed in this world? Nothing. Reality is reality. We are each human beings that need a place to live. We need to eat and drink. We need to find a way to pay for ourselves as we pass through life. We may even need love and family relationships. That is real. Everything else is simply illusion. It is only words.

Like I frequently say, in my lifetime, I have met so many fake gurus, clairvoyants, psychics, people who claim they can talk to the angels, conjure up the dead, you name it… But, it is all bullshit. They are all bullshit.

I have also met many a true believer; true yogis, true monks, who live in the most pure, simply way possible, and claim no greater gift than that they are walking the path of whatever god they believe in. They claim nothing, they sell nothing, they need far less than you or I. They are what is real with the world of metaphysics. But, these people are few in numbers compared to those who are out there claiming mystical powers.

Everybody wants to be a superhero. But, nobody can be so what is left? What is left is the claim of spiritual powers that no one can test.

If you have the mind for it, you can always see the patterns that a psychic uses when they meet someone and try to tell them about whatever it is that person wants to know. They ask questions. The moment a question is rebuked they go forward in another direction until they receive an answer that they can build upon. You don't have to go to a psychic to witness this, watch it on TV. These people are very skilled in their abilities of human observation and how to direct a conversation. Again, this brings us to psychology verse parapsychology.

What is here, what is now, what you are feeling, and how you are living is real; that is what matters. The only reason you look to the great beyond and to the people who claim that they can guide you there, the only reason any of us do, is because we are not satisfied with our life; we want something more: be it a person, money, position, power, knowledge, or happiness. We want something that we do not have. Thus, all metaphysics is based upon is human need—therefore all spirituality is based upon psychology. …If you are happy and fulfilled, you do not look to the heavens.

Now, it is very true, there is great wisdom that has been passed down through the ages in the various religious scriptures. What they all teach is basically the same thing: be good, do good, and do not be controlled by desire. You don't need a guru or a psychic to tell you that. All you need to do is practice the teachings of whatever faith you hold.

The various schools of metaphysics may be fun but it is far more easy to become lost in the lie(s) that they teach then to gain enlightenment through the realization of the simply truths of life. Let go of desire and you are free. Let go of seeking prestige and you are free. Let go of believing that you do not have enough and you are free. Let go of believing that you know more than anyone else, that you are better than anyone else, and you are free. Let go of the lie that somebody has something that they can give you from the great beyond and you are free.

So, why psychology over parapsychology? Because it is real. I call it, *"Humanology."*

Be real. Live real. Embrace the real. Be nice. Be helpful. Do good things. Hurt no one. And, that is as good as your life can be.

When You Find Out You've Been Following the Wrong Path
05/Dec/2016 09:45 AM

The majority of the world's populous lacks true human awareness. They care about what they are feeling but they do not care about what you are feeling. Some people are drawn to the path of rising human consciousness. But why? Most simply do this because they want something more for their life. They want to understand. They want to be more. They want to have more. They do not do it because they want to find out a better method to help humanity. They do it for themselves.

The majority of the world's people are very selfish creatures. When they do give, they give because giving makes them look good in the eyes of other people—they give because giving makes them feel good. Thus, they are receiving something for their actions. Is this giving at all?

Many people are indoctrinated into religious beliefs from their early years forward. Others, turn to religion and/or spirituality and self-help when they reach a point in their life when things are not going in the direction that they had hoped.

At the root of all religion is making the world a better place through the belief in something—by following the teachings of those immaculate beings that have walked the earth before us. But, how many people who turn to religion do so as a means of achieving the greater universal good through true giving with no judgment attached? Most, simply find solace by belonging to and interacting with a group consciousness of, *"I am this!"* This mindset obviously gives birth to personal kinship but not to universal enlightenment.

Then, there are those who step to the pulpit. They (personally) believe they have something to teach. But, what is at the root of any teacher? Ego. *"I have something to teach. You have something to learn."* Many teachers exclaim, *"I am doing this to help people."* But, are they? And, who are they truly helping? Are the truly helping other people or are they only helping themselves because their ego is being filled by developing a following?

Any person who has the ego to believe that they have something to teach has completely missed the point of spiritual education. Enlightenment comes from within. Spiritual understanding arises from individualized knowledge. It can never be taught. It can never be given. Thus, all a spiritual teacher is doing is stroking their own ego. This is why so many of them hit the wall of failure. This is why so many of them encounter professional and financial demise. Why? Because they have believed their own lie that they have inner-knowledge to teach and thus, while being guided solely by their ego, they damaged the lives of others.

But, what happens to you, the individual who seeks a deeper understanding of life and the universe when you realize that what you believed in was not the truth—what and who you believed in turned out to be a lie?

In fact, this is a common occurrence in all areas of life. Whether is was a personal relationship that went south—you believed in the person but what they promised turned out to be a lie, an employer that really messed with your life when all you hoped for was a good job, onto a belief in a project, an association, a school, a group, or a religious organization that turned out to be a total disaster. …You believed. You worked for that larger whole. But, at the end of the day, you were cheated out of what was promised. Now what?

Many people at this point in their life immediately try to seek out another THAT of whatever it was they were previously involved with. Whether this is the rebound relationship or trying to merge with the larger whole of some other grouping of people; many try to find sanctuary by doing exactly what they did before—looking out there instead of looking in here.

The fact is, being part of a large whole is very consoling. There is always someone who will pretend to listen to you so that you can commiserate with them. But, what does this do for the greater good of the universe? How does this help you become whole onto yourself? Yes, you may find a new mate. You may find a new organization. You may be filled with distraction. But what happens when the same thing happens? ...When what you were promised does not come to be a reality.

Here's the thing... As long as you seek out there, you will forever be disappointed. As long as you believe in someone or something, there will come a time when who and/or what you believed in will let you down. As stated in this binging of this discourse, most people lack true human awareness. When they are put to test, they will choose themselves—they will choose what is good for them long before they ever choose what is good for you.

Think about you... How many times have you chosen them over you? How many times have you choosing to let go of whatever it is you want and truly give in to what that other person wants? Very few times I would imagine. This is the basis of human reality. You can pretend it does not exist but it does.

Yes, people give in to loved ones and to people in control when they hope to gain something from the giving. But, that is not giving. That is getting by giving. And getting by giving is never true giving.

Again, this brings us back to YOU. If you hope to GET by being with someone, being a part of something, or believing in something, you will be disappointed. Thus, if you hope to find a true whole in yourself—if you hope to find ultimate fulfillment never give into the belief that THAT will get you THIS.

You want to be free? Believe in no-one and no-thing.

The People Who Never Evolve
04/Dec/2016 04:40 PM

Life is a process of personal evolution. We are born, we experience, we are taught, and we continue to pass from birth to death; growing in both understanding and in wisdom. Many of us have done foolish things when we were young. When we look back to those times, we shake our heads and question, *"How could I have ever been so unwise?"* But, we have grown, we have evolved, we have become better people—we took a long hard look at our self, our life, we studied our existence, we learned from our mistakes, and we emerged as a better person refusing to ever make the same mistakes again.

Not everyone is like this, however. There are some people who never change—they never evolve. They are so lost in the realms of misplaced self-adsorption that they never take the time to learn from their mistakes and to understand that bad thoughts, bad words, and bad deeds not only do nothing to help the overall evolution of this world but they, in fact, hold them back, (as a person), from ever achieving anything of substance with their life.

Having been involved in the martial arts for over fifty years, I have watched as many so-called martial artists have played the game of attempting to make themselves, their teacher, their school, or their system look like something more by diminishing the accomplishments of others. Throughout these years I have watched as most of these people have grown into something more—became something better and have left this foolishness behind. But, this is not the case of everyone. Every now and then I will encounter a person, years later, and discover that they are still locked into the mindset of believing that it somehow makes them look like something more if they say something negative or bad (be it truth or a lie) about someone else. I forever find this very-very sad. The martial arts are about making someone a better; more whole, more complete person. The martial arts should never be diminished to the level of personal attack—motived by individual ego. This type or behavior destroys the true essence of the martial arts. It robs them of their true beauty, as this type of behavior is simply motivated by a very sad and low level of human consciousness.

Having been involved in the film business for the past three decades, I often encountered this type of behavior, as well. The one thing I will say is that the film business is an industry motivated by ego. So, unlike the martial arts, which should solely be about focusing on the higher self, the motivation for this behavior can be more understood in this arena of life. This is not to say it is right or good, but it can be explained.

The fact is, it is easy to find a reason for criticism in the film industry. You may not like a performance, a storyline, or a style of cinematography. From this, judgments are made.

Certainly, the enlightened filmmaker does not follow this path. As a true filmmaker, they understand that each project and/or actor is art onto itself. The true filmmaker understands that whether or not they personally like a specific project, that project is simply a process of giving to the great whole of the art form. Thus, judgment is put aside.

But, as in all things in life, the low-minded, the unaware, the egotistical, and the unaccomplished are generally the ones who are screaming the loudest.

Over the recent years I have found myself discussing the internet and how it relates to human consciousness quite frequently. The internet is the defining factor of this period of history. As such, it has become the conduit for both all that is good and all that is bad with humankind. From this, many have found a voice where in times gone past they would have had none.

Here, on this internet, people can say anything about anyone with little consequence. Most hide behind screen names so no one even knows who or what they truly are. To me, this simply seems like a coward's soapbox. People scream as loud as they can; scream about anyone or anything but they do not even have the personal level of Self-Honor to tell the world who is truly saying what, what they have accomplished in their life that gives the the right to voice an opinion, and why they are saying it in the first place.

This brings us back to the entire point of this discourse. Most of us evolve as we pass through life. We become more, we become better, we develop a deeper understanding of life and, from this, we possess less unfounded critical judgment. We, through our own personal accomplishments and our own mental evolution, become more whole onto ourselves. Instead of issuing critiques, criticism, and deformation, we reach out a helping hand. We want to make the world a better place. We want to help those that need help. We do not want to hurt anyone in anyway for any reason. But, the sad truth of life is, some people never evolve. They have become so lost in their interpersonal anger, the sense of unfulfilment, their lack of personal accomplishment that they remain lost in the mind of attack. From this, all that they do is attack, especially when they can hide behind the wall of perceived anonymity.

For those of us of who walk the path of consciousness, we cannot allow ourselves to be drawn into their web of misplace anger—anger that should be focused on themselves for behaving in an uncivilized manner but, instead, is broadcast to the world. These people are out there and you will, more than likely, encounter them. When you do, the best course of action is understanding and forgiveness. Forgive them, because if they were not a truly lost person they would not be doing what they do.

At each stage of our life we all need took at ourselves. We need to view what we have done: whom we have helped and whom we have hurt. We need to study our own personal trajectory. Where are we going in our life? What will be the consequences of the actions we are currently performing?

Many people hide from the truth of their life. They hide as many do on the internet. They believe the actions issued by a screen name are not true and their will be no ensuing karma leveled at them because of these seemingly anonymous deeds. This is, however, the explanation of the unaware and the unenlightened.

Everything you do sets everything else in motion. Whether people know who you truly are or they only see a screen name is virtually irreverent. What you have done is what you have done. What you have said is what you have said. If what you have done or what you have said does not produce immediate positive reaction your world will be negatively influenced. This is why so many people fail in life, because what they are doing is not adding to the greater good.

People fall prey to the addiction that can be had from the adrenaline of unleashing negative emotions outwards. But, take a moment and study that emotion. What are you experiencing when you embrace that negative emotion? Is it positive? No, it is anger and it is rage. Does anything positive ever come from of anger and rage? No, it does not.

Now, think about this, if you have spread that anger and rage outwards, perhaps on the internet, think how many people are encountering your anger and your rage. What do you think will come from that? What you have done is set a negative course of events into motion and those negative events may be wide spanning. Yes, maybe your ego was stoked because you said or did something to someone or something that you do not like. But, that is you unleashing your personal judgment—which is egotism. And, we all know what happens to those who base their life upon egotism. Thus, ultimately, what have you done? At best, you found a moment of ego stimulation and a momentary adrenaline rush. In the long run, however, you set a course of negative events into motion which will, sooner-or-later, all come back to haunt you.

Now, to the evolved person, they will immediately understand and agree with this. To the unevolved they will argue in their mind and defend their right to say or do anything that they feel like. …The world and its people be damned.

But now, for those of you who behave in this manner, let's look at your life. Is your life all that you hoped it would be? I would bet that it is not. And, that is probably why you are embracing your unevolved mindset. You are angry at what you are not.

Again, let's look at you. You can turn this around. Yes, it can be addicting to spew out negativity. But, if you are not living the life that you want to live, then what is that addiction giving you? Just like all additions, it is harming you. Stop it! Be more! Do more! Undo the negativity you have created and redo it with the positive!

Your life can be more. It can be what you want it to be. But, you have to make it that way by not allowing yourself to be seduced by the negative and doing only positive things.

And So, What Have You Done with Your Life?
03/Dec/2016 08:11 AM

"*And so, what have you done with your life?*" This is a question that each person should be asking themselves. And, the fact of the matter is, the way you ask this question of yourself (and of others) truly can put specific emphasis on the way the question can and will be answered.

...This is a question that each person should be asking themselves but very few people do. Instead, they prefer to go to the mindset of attack mode and set about finding fault with what others have done instead of truly taking a long, hard look at themselves and actually witness what they are creating in their life and the lives of others with whom they interact.

It is an unfortunate component of the human condition that people decide to talk about and/or judge what others have done instead of viewing the way they, personally, are encountering life. The fact is, judgment is easy. Setting about on a specified course and actually accomplishing something is so much harder. But, the people who live their life from a position of judgment refuse to realize this. Instead, they gain personal self-satisfaction by lashing out at others; as it so much easier than actually accomplishing something/doing something that truly matters.

If you study people, when someone is young they are commonly filled with great ideals about what their life will equal. As they begin to grow older, and the realities of life set in—the fact that there is a cost to living, there are bills to pay, and people must take responsibility for their own desires, their own actions, and the consequences of what these desires and actions have instigated sets in. From this, instead of becoming more motivated to actually focus on and achieve their dreams, many become more-and-more negative through the passing of time and, with this, they become bitter. Some begin to sink to the lower levels of humanity and embrace drink, drugs, and physical or verbal violence. From this, they enter a downward spiral and become lost in the negativity that they, themselves, have orchestrated.

Of course, no one will admit this about themselves. At least not out loud. But, the fact of the what they do and the what they speak becomes self-evident as it clearly depicts the life path they are embracing and living. From this mode of behavior, personal accomplishments become harder and harder to actualize as negativity has engulfed their life.

Each person, as they pass through life, has a unique set of desires they wish to accomplish. The fact is, most of us will never achieve all of the desires we hold near to our heart. This being said, this does not mean that we cannot move towards their achievement in a positive and directed manner.

What people never seem to realize is that each word of negativity they unleash, each actions of negative they unleash holds them back from embracing not only their true, better-self but it also keeps them from become the whole and perfect expression of themselves. It keeps them from accomplishment. It keeps them from becoming what they hoped for their life. The reason for this is simple, if you raise yourself up, embracing negativity, all you have is an unsubstantiated footing and you will fall.

It is for this reason that it is essential to never base your life upon what you are not by judging what someone else is. For by doing this you never become any-anything— you simply become a conduit for judgment and negativity and this is never a some-thing. It is only a means to propel others to greater heights of notoriety by drawing attention to them while you make yourself look smaller by causing others to believe you have nothing better to discuss than the life of someone else.

What is the answer then? The answer is to focus on becoming what you truly hope to become and do this based in your own sense of positivity while giving back to the greater good of the world.

As I say over-and-over again, negativity never equals anything positive—judgment never does anything but casts a negative focus on you while shining the light on someone else.

You may never become what you truly hope to become. This is the fact of life that we all must face. But, if you can keep your focus on the positive and be the best that you can be while hurting or damaging no one else in the process—then, at the end of your days, you can say that you lived a good life. And, that is all any of us can truly hope for. That is the only thing that we can guarantee as we are the one who is totally in control of what we say and what we do.

Live a good life then all else will come to you naturally.

Your Life Does Not Matter
02/Dec/2016 11:50 AM

I was going to have breakfast this morning at a restaurant I frequent. There were two tables available outside—rain or shine, heat or cold, I always prefer to eat outside when I can. I went inside and ordered; got my food and coffee and was heading out the door. Just as I was, two females sat down at one of the tables and an elderly man sat down at the other. None of them had ordered any food or drink... They just wanted to sit at the table(s). So, there I was; food in hand and no where to sit. With do other choice, I headed for my car...

Did those people ever consider that they had come between the life-plans of another person? Did they care? Probably not... Do you care what happens to me? Probably not... Do you care what happens to anybody in their life? Probably not... At most, you only care about the people you care about and you only care about them because they do something for you or make you feel a certain way.

This is an essential thing to think about as you pass through life... Who do you care about and why? And, who don't you care about?

Ponder this... How much time do you spend thinking about anyone but yourself? Sure, you may spend a lot of time daydreaming about a person you wish to be in a relationship with. You may think about someone who has something you want. You may even attempt to present yourself as some sort of expert about a specific sports player or celebrity—so you spend all kinds of time researching them... But, all of that energy is based upon desire. You want something from someone or you want to be seen as knowing the most about a specific person or persons. You only care about them because they have something you want. You only care about them because they have something to offer you.

I would claim that is not caring at all. All the emotions you are experiences towards that person or persons simply involves you getting what you want. But, caring… Who do you truly care about?

Sure, you may care about that one person… But, what about everybody else—all the other people in the world? Do you care at all?

Have you ever taken the seat that someone was planning to sit in? If you did, did you care? If you did, were you even aware enough to notice that you took the seat that someone else was about to sit down in? If someone said, *"Hey, I was planning to sit there."* Did you say, *"Sorry,"* and get up and leave? Or, did you just simply become angry at them and them to, *"Fuck off?"*

Now, ponder this… Who cares about you? And, why do they care about you? What are you giving them that makes them care? If you stopped giving them that thing, (whatever that thing may be), would they still care about you?

The fact of life is; your life does not matter. The majority of the world does not care about you at all. Certainly, there are some people who rise to the top of the game and truly do something positive—they truly do something helpful to the greater whole of humanity. But, is that you? Do you even try to give anything back to the all of humanity? And, if you do, is what you are giving based upon you truly caring or is it based upon your ego—trying to make yourself look like something more than the average person?

…Selflessness never involves your ego.

Again, who do you care about and why? Again, who cares about you and why?

Ultimately, your life is defined by what you say about other people, what you think about other people, and how you behave towards other people.

Do you care enough to care? Or, are you so locked into your own sense of self-worth that all you think about is

how you are feeling in a particular moment—what you are doing in a particular moment, and who is doing what to you?
Face it, your life does not matter.

Most People Don't Have the Desire to Win
13/Nov/2016 10:42 AM

People forever want what they want. To each person this is a unique commodity. They want what they want, they want it to happen, but they do not possess the fortified desire to make it a reality.

People listen to the words of all the personality gurus who speak and speak about achieving your dreams. They listen, they believe, they want, they think, they fantasize, but they do nothing to make it a reality.

Fantasy is easy. It takes no real effort.

At the sourcepoint of all desire is YOU. You are the one who wants something. It almost does not even matter what you want. For wanting is one thing—everybody wants but few do anything about what they want.

For those who do, this is where all of the problems begin.

What you want is what you want. Okay… What are you going to do to achieve it? As stated, most people do nothing. But, then there are those who do something. Most, if they do anything at all, do it in the most half-assed manner. They only try as long as their ego is being feed in the process of trying but then there comes a time when they either realize what their desire is unhaveable—undoable or they desire something else. Thus, they leave the desire for its achievement behind—cast to the realms of, *"Who I used to be."*

For those who want a particular something, many seek out a teacher. There are teachers everywhere. It seems everyone has something to say. But, few can claim that they have truly walked down a specific road long enough to actually be considered a teacher. Most who talk have no right to talk because they have not earned the right to talk. Thus, all they do is mess up the life of those they talk to.

It is far easier to be a self-proclaimed teacher and charge people for your services than to have actually accomplished something.

Spiritual teachers are everywhere. It's easy, there is no license to achieve. There is no place where you go and have to pass a test. Pundits all have something to say. Talk is easy/talk is cheap. But, the true teacher, the one who has actually accomplished something and has true knowledge to offer, those are hard to come by. …Hard to come by but they are out there.

Again, here lies one of the biggest problems on the road to achieving what you desire… It is almost guaranteed that you are not the only one desiring what you desire. The more people who desire some specific something, the more false profits there are in the field promising you that they can guide you to it.

Everybody lies. This is one of the key facts you must understand in life before you ever try to pursue anything. If someone cannot document their exact accomplishments in whatever field they claim to hold knowledge about, they are nothing more than another liar.

So, in your process to achievement you must first know exactly what you want. Then, you must be willing to pay the price to achieve it. And remember, there is always a high price to pay in the pursuit of achieving any desire. Are you willing to pay it?

Once you have your desire clearly in mind, can you focus your entire life on achieving it? Can you do what it takes to make it happen?

Many people claim to be something that they are not. This, again, goes back to the fact that everybody lies. Who are you? Are you a liar? If you are, that is all you will ever be? Or, can you forgo your ego, forgo who you want the world to believe that you are and truly BE in your becoming?

We all want something. Who are you? What are you? And, what are you willing to do to actually achieve the truth in your self-fantasy?

I Believe: Compounding Factual Inaccuracies
05/Nov/2016 07:56 AM

Life is based upon a set of beliefs. These beliefs come to us from many sources. We gain them from what we are taught, what we hear and read, what we witness, and then; once we have been provided with a certain set of parameters given to us by our culture, our desires, and our placement in life and time, we decide what we believe.

Some people decide what they believe and then simply do the conscious thing; believe it. Others decide it is they who have the calling, the desire, the ability, the power, the gift, and/or the need to broadcast their beliefs to the world. From this, they spread their ideologies out, from within in their own mind, to others. Why do they do this? The simple answer is ego. They want to be seen as a knower. If they are not seen as a knower then, at least, they believe they will be understood to be a discontent, sewing the seeds of controversy and anarchy.

There is one essential problem is the conception of, *"I believe,"* however. Belief is opinion, it is not fact.

In a free society every one has the right to have their opinion. But, if a person lives a life of consciousness they understand that their, *"Opinion,"* is just that—it is not a fact. It is simply what they believe and belief is an interpersonal process, it is not a factual accounting of reality and something that someone should expound outwards to the world for then only one thing occurs; the compounding of factual inaccuracies which have the potential to negatively affect the life of others.

It is like the conspiracy theorists, they look for and try to find logical reasoning for what they believe to be an anomaly of life, time, space, and/or occurrences. But, there is fact and then there is theory. Some people attempt to broadcast their theories to the minds of other people. This does not make their ideologies fact; it simply makes them broadcasted theories. And, each theory is simply some-thing that a particular some-one hopes to make fact based upon what they, personally, believe. It is not fact, however, it is simply belief. Yet, they hope to pull others into the web of what they believe. This is how many of the falsehood that have been disseminated through societies, throughout time, have come to take hold. Not fact, simply belief that a large number of people have come to believe.

The fact is, some people are so locked into their beliefs that even if you present them with factual evidence that what they believe is wrong they will argue with you about the validity of your presentation and will not concede that their belief about a practical subject and/or their belief system in general may be wrong.

Some people become very lost between the concept of opinion and fact. If they do not possess an analytical mind they simply assume that there is no difference. People driven by ego, desire, jealousy, or anger often fall prey to their own undefined differences between these two mental concepts. They believe, so what they believe IS. But, is it? Is your belief ever the defining truth for the entire world? Yes, it may be the defining truth for your world but should your belief be expounded to others? Do you ever ponder this fact before you spread your belief(s) outwards?

How much of your life mind-time do you spend pondering the fact of understanding where your belief system arose? How much of your life mind-time do you spend actually contemplating why you are saying, what you are saying, when you are disseminating your beliefs outwards, beyond yourself? When you do speak of your beliefs do you only care about the fact that you desire your beliefs to be witnessed as the truth? In fact, do you ever think at all before you speak of your belief? Finally, what is your desired end result when you propagate your belief? Why do you discuss your belief(s) at all? These are all important concepts to think about as you pass through life.

It is essential to contemplate why you believe what you believe. Think about this, have you ever believed one thing and now you believe it no more? This is the simple formula to help you define for yourself the difference between belief or fact. And, it is also essential to keep in mind, just because other people believe something (even large groups of people like a religion) this does that mean that you are forced to believe it?

Belief is only what it is; an ideology formed in your own mind. As long as it is kept in your own mind, it can hurt no one. As soon as it is released chaos is given birth to.

Belief is never fact.

All the Art that is Lost
31/Oct/2016 01:22 PM

I was in the LBC visiting an old friend. When I left I realized there was some construction going on so instead of taking the street I normally drive down I drove through the alley to bypass the traffic jam. As I was driving through the alley I noticed that there was this really nice piece of art leaning against a trash can. I stopped and looked at it.

Looking, I realized it was actually two pieces of spray paint art. They were done on two closet doors. As this was in the back of an apartment building, I assume what happened is that the artist moved out and the landlord, caring not about the art, took down the doors and threw them away.

The artist was really good. It was a combination of a portrait and some more abstract work. I didn't have room in my car to pack them up and take them with me but I did take a couple of photographs. Hopefully, that will help that art live on forever.

Seeing the art laying there, awaiting the garbage truck, it really set me to thinking. I mean, think about it, how much of the world's art has been lost to people who do not care about art?

The fact is, very few people care about art. Fewer yet are the artists who create the art. Pretty much everybody has an opinion about art. Everybody wants to criticize art. But, criticism is easy. It takes no vision, no focus, no creativity. It only takes judgment.

Sure, everybody has an opinion; we all like what we like, dislike what we don't. But, most people, at best, use their opinions about art as a way of demeaning someone else. But, why does their opinion even matter? What have they created? The fact is, through their words, all they have done is unleashed negativity out to the world. Negativity is never art.

All of this really comes down to the question(s) of, *"Who are you? What do you do? Do you contribute to the every-expanding art of the world? Or, do you simply wrongly believe that your opinion matters more than the actual creation(s) of the artist?"* If you believe the ladder, it demonstrates you possess a very limited, judgmental, and selfish mindset. If you are not the artist, you can never understand the artist's motivations and artistic reality surround the creation of their art. Thus, who are you to say anything?

Art is what gives this world meaning. It defines life, culture, and a space in time. What do you contribute?

Wild in the Streets
31/Oct/2016 01:15 PM

I'm sure I have used this for a title in the past—referencing that great piece of 60's cinema but it again, very-descriptively, details a couple of my recent encounters...

I was driving down a side street the other day and I was pulling into the left turn lane. Just as I did a guy, in his new SUV, jams out of a parking lot and comes straight for me. I stop. He stops. I smile and point, indicating that I am trying to make a left turn. He completely goes off. I mean he was yelling and screaming, telling me, *"Fuck you!"* But why? Why was he so angry? It was he who had made an illegal maneuver. I was just trying to turn left. Yet, his anger dominated his every emotion. Finally, he screeches his tires and pulls out and around me and speeds down the street still yelling.

A couple of week ago I was coming home from the studio. It was a bit before total traffic time; maybe 4:00 or 4:30. I was again driving down a semi-side street that I know to avoid some of the L.A. traffic. I pulled up to a red light behind a few other cars. A guy, driving another SUV, wants to turn right but there is not enough room for him to pass due to the design of the lanes on the street. He starts honking and yelling at me. *"Fuck you! I'll kill you, you mutha fucker,"* he screams. Me, who always tries to be very conscious of other drivers, I couldn't pull up any closer to the car in front of me than I already was. Finally, he drives over the curb and plows his was through. But, why? Why was he so angry?

Now, there is certainly a place in me, that urban kid who has been somewhat unable to leave my years of ghetto life behind, that is more than willing to get out of my car and go toe-to-toe when somebody comes at me like this. But, I always try to focus on my higher self. And hey, I am fifty-eight years old now, so I shouldn't be street fighting. ☺ But, more than that, I truly wonder why these people are so angry at life? What is so wrong with their life that they are so out of control of their emotions? I mean, these are the kind of people you have to really watch out for because they are the ones who are so locked into a state of emotional upheaval that they can guide your life down a dark road by churning the emotions of your lower self and bringing you into their world disassociated anger.

Think about this world… There is some really messed up stuff going on right now. Think about all the ruination of the many-many lives that is taking place in the Middle East. And, though that is the primary focus of the right now, there is always some crazy shit going on somewhere. These people are truly suffering. Their lives are being destroyed. They have a reason to be angry. Not someone driving in a new SUV.

This kind of raging, out of control, mentality was brought very clearly into my life a few years ago when I had a neighbor move in who would just go off the handle and scream, *"Fuck me, Fuck me, Fuck me and mine!"* He did this over and over and over again as he stomped on the floor like a four-year-old. And, this guy was my age. He totally destroyed the life and the lifestyle of all of the neighbors around him, including me. It was the kind of self-created action that equaled devastation in that it is still felt even today because he ruined a lot of the time then that equals the time now. He ruined the what should have been. None of us asked for that. None of us wanted that. Life was fine before he moved in. Did I or did any of us ever get an apology? Did he ever try to undo the damage he created? No. His only response, when I finally spoke with him was, *"Everybody gets angry."* Sure we do. We all get pissed. But, most of us have developed the ability to be in control of our emotions and not let them unwantedly enter into and destroy the lives of others. We don't broadcast them to the world. We control them as opposed to them controlling us.

Luckily, I eventually moved and the guys in the two SUV drove on. But, it is those people who are the ones who enter a person's life and can really mess it up.

Certainly, I have known various people throughout my years who have had issues with anger. Some had diagnosed mental illness and they took their meds. Some were undiagnosed and just raged. But in each case, in each person's life, it is they who must be self-aware enough of what is going on with them and what effect they are having on the world around that they consciously look at themselves and do something about who they are and how they are behaving. I have had to do that with my life as I think we all have done when we realize that the way we are behaving is not conducive to the great good of the world around us. I mean, come on, what is so bad with your life, living in a great and free society, that you must inflict your anger onto other people and damage their life? What gives you that right?

And, this is not simply focused solely on people with anger issues. There are the hurtful, the jealous, the envious, the unthinking, the uncaring, the seekers of melodrama, and the psycho bitches. Each of these mind-types have the potential to bring devastation to the life of other people.

Ultimately, there is really nothing you can do about it. People are who people are. Not all of us live our lives consciously. And, I am sure in each of the aforementioned cases the individual would have a reason (most likely an excuse) for behaving the way that they behave. The thing is, as I always say, life begins with you. Not only your life but the life of all those you encounter is defined by the choices you make and the actions you take. So, what you do, you must do with a sense of formalized consciousness. …A consciousness that is not solely focused on you and how you feel. You must forever be in control of yourself. You must be more than your emotions. This is not only the pathway to enlightenment but it is the pathway to making the world a better place.

Not of Our Culture
15/Oct/2016 09:22 AM

Cultural indoctrination is a really interesting process in that where we are formed is where we learn how to behave and from that we go through life behaving in a very specific manner. Now, this is all fine and good if you spend your entire life living in one culture (or subculture) and never step outside beyond its boundaries. But, if you do move away from YOUR culture into an another culture, you must adapt. If you do not, then all you do is create havoc, chaos, and discomfort in the lives of those you come into contact with. This discomfort can be small or it can be large. It can be a simple annoyance or it can create a life changing event. But, the one common factor in all of this is that one or more person(s) enters into the realm of another and if they behave in a culturally unacceptable manner, the person or persons whose life they have entered is altered for the worst.

How do you behave? Do you take your culture with you or do you adapt to the culture around you?

It is important to preface this writing with the fact that I am not demeaning any culture. Just the opposite, in fact. But, the fact of the matter is, cultural adaptation, guiding by the blending of cultures, ideally takes place over long periods of time. If someone attempts to immediately pressure cultural adaption by forcing their cultural beliefs into the place they newly have come to inhabit, then conflict is given birth to.

I have spent much of my adult life traveling the globe. Many years ago the foreigners I would encounter, while abroad, were most commonly Americans. This is not the case anymore. Due to the overall demise of the U.S. economy and other factors, it is much more likely that you will encounter a traveler from another region of the world than America. The point being, it used to almost be a joke about the way Americans would behave in other countries.

Even me, I was embarrassed by the way they acted and would have nothing to do with them. They expected that the world should be just the way it is in America—that all those across the globe should behave in a manner that the American mindset deemed appropriate and due to the fact that they were, *"American,"* they should be kowtowed to. Very sad. Very inappropriate. But, this is how some people behave.

Even me, I remember the first time I travel to Berlin, (back when it was West Berlin), my German was very poor. I went to the post office to mail a package and I tired to communicate with the postal worker in English. He scolded me, yelled ay me, told me to learn German and I totally got it. This was his country. German was their language and I couldn't speak it very well. Finally, he changed his tone and spoke to me in perfect English. But, it was my fault. Not his.

From an American perspective, in the recent decades, large numbers of immigrates have immigrated into the United States. Many, if not most, have come here hoping to be a part of the American culture. But, some have not. Though they are here, they wish to hold-fast to their own culture and simply reap the rewards of America. From this, I have witnessed conflict, disharmony, and distrust arise. For example, in the area of Los Angeles where I live there is a lot of new money and a lot of old family money. I have watched as large numbers of people of Middle-Eastern heritage have come to the area and completely disregarding common cultural courtesies. For example, I think back to a time recently when I was sitting outdoors at a Starbucks. As we all know Starbucks is a smoke-free environment. This one guy drove his top of the line BMW up and parked right in front of the shop in the red zone. He didn't care... Went and got a coffee, came outside and lighted up a cigarette and started blowing smoke. This, even though there is a no-smoking badge on the table where he sat. Now, I really hate conflict. I think most of us do. But, was I going to let this man ruin this environment for the old guy, the high school girls, and myself sitting on this patio? No. I straight-away went up to him and told him about the rules and told him he was being very rude. But, he knew and he didn't care. He was just going to push the boundaries as far as he could and the rest of the world be damned. Smoking was who he is. He looked at me. He said nothing. He went and sat in his car, parked in the red, drank his coffee, and smoked his cigarette.

This is just one small example about how people (culturally) invade the space of others. In his culture smoking everywhere/anywhere is fine. But, not here. But, he didn't care. Though it all turned out fine and that was good. This is not always the case, however. This man unconsciously created conflict simply by bringing his culture with him and not caring about the culture of the land where he now resides. And, creating conflict, based upon cultural indoctrination, is never a good thing.

In various articles and in the various incarnations of this Zen Blog and in other places, I have detained how periodically people have come into my life, uninvited, and really messed it up. They have done this because they were inconsiderate of my life and the life of other people and/or maybe they just did not care. In some cases, when confronted about what they had done, they have sited reasons like that was they way they learned to behave where they were from and nonsensical excuses such as that. But, the fact is, they came in and damaged my life—they damaged the life of others. And, they did this because they were not aware enough, not conscious enough, to care. And this takes us to the heart of the matter. In life, we each move from place to place. Whether this is miles upon miles or simply across town, in each of these places we find people who behave in a certain manner and they expect to be treated in a specific manner. If you behave differently, if you act wrongly, if you go into their space and do something that negatively affects the life of anybody; you are in the wrong. It is a simple as that. And, if you do wrong things, that hurts the lives of other people, based upon how you believe it is okay to behave, you are the one causing the problem. Thus, all the blame goes to you.

Now, the fact is, some people don't care. They take their culture with them wherever they go and the world be damned. But, that mindset is the cause of conflict. That is where all the fights, all the wars, and all of the problems of the world begin. Is that how you behave?

What are you the sourcepoint of and for? Do you care more about meaninglessly holding onto the bad habits of your culture or do you care about caring enough to care about others first? You really need to ask yourself that question whenever you find yourself in a new environment. Do you adapt? Or, do you pollute?

There's Millions of People Who Are Suffering
15/Aug/2016 09:20 AM

Have you even gotten into the shower and the water was too cold? Have you ever taken a shower and the water was too hot? Though you take a shower in the same place everyday, for some reason, on this day, you just have a very hard time getting the water just right.

I think back to one of the times I was in Burma. I was twenty-five and I was staying at the only hotel that was in existence, at the time, in Mandalay. I had woken up one morning and I went to hit the shower before I went out to the day. The water pressure was *ify,* the temperature of the water was inconsistent, the floor of the shower was a cold cement basin, and it was all making me really frustrated. Anyway, finishing my shower, having my breakfast in the hotel restaurant, I went out and was walking around the streets. As I was, I saw several of the locals taking their morning shower/bath. They were in front or to the side of their small wooden homes. What they had was a bucket full of water that they would dip their washcloth or a sponge into and wash themselves down with it. One guy, when he was done, took the bucket and poured it over his head. That was his shower. I wondered how the he liked the temperature and/or the water pressure?

Here's the point, there are so many people out there who do not have any of the comforts that we do. Yet, we are the one's complaining. We are the one's obsessing about some-thing, some object that we desire, or some person. We are doing all we can for what WE want but we are nothing for anyone else. We are not thinking about anyone else but ourselves.

What do you do to help the people who are suffering? What do you do to help the people, across the globe, that actually need help? Do you spend you time mentally masturbating on the internet or do you get off of your ass and go out and do something that actual help someone who needs help?

If you do not take your mental focus off of yourself and what you want to do when you want to do it, your life is meaningless. If you do not get out there and do something positive, and actually helpful, to make the lives of those in-need better, your life is meaningless. If you focus your energy on hurting anyone, no matter what your motivation, instead of helping someone/everyone, your life is meaningless.

People are in need all around us. You don't have to go to Burma to find them. There are millions of people who are suffering, are you one of them? Probably not. If you are not, then get out there and help someone. Get out of your own head and do something good. For this is the only true measure of a person. This is the only thing that you can actually take pride in accomplishing. This is the only thing that all humanity will actually applaud. The only thing that truly matters in life is, who are you helping, who's life are you making better, and who's life have you removed pain from?

Today's a good day to start. Get off your butt and go out and do something that actually helps someone.

How You Handle It
15/Aug/2016 09:20 AM

Life is defined by events. Events: large or small, are defined by what you have done in your life and how you have reacted to previous events. A person's life is defined by an ever-growing string of events and how they have reacted to or handled each of them.

In life, we are each deal a set of cards that defines who and what we can become. Some of us are lucky and are born in the Free World where an individual's choice of religion, philosophy, occupation, and whom they will be in a relationship with is made solely by the person. Some are born lucky and they are given birth to in a happy home where their parents and the surrounding community are supportive and nurturing. Some are lucky and they are born with no psychiatric or physiologic detriments. Yet, do all of the people who are born with these obvious life advantages walk forward through their life making the right choices that hurt no one and handle their life events is a positive, productive manner? The answer to that question is obviously, no. And, this is where the chaos for an individual's personal life and the effect they have on the lives of others is set into motion. This is where all the problems of the world are either created and/or are put to rest.

As stated, life is defined by events. Each day we each encounter a series of life events. These life events are largely defined by the choices we have made in relationship to the life we have hoped to live and, as such, we are the one who was the instigator of what life events we will most likely next encounter.

Where you have chosen to live, what you have chosen to do, what desires fill your mind, whom you have chosen to associate with—all of these elements come to define the events you will encounter in life.

Many people seek only a simple existence: a job that they like, a community where they enjoy living, and associating with people of like mind. They define their world based upon what was and is available to them, presented by where they find themselves in terms of time, history, and society.

There is the innate need in all people to be in a relationship with a person and persons and survive within in those relationships in a healthy, happy, and productive manner. The desire for this natural human interaction is what sets a good percentage of a person's life events into motion. The desire for interaction, and the price one pays to have this, will often come to define much of a person's life.

Human interaction is both good and it is bad. It has the potential to do great things for an individual. It also has the potential to be very damaging. Human interaction is the sourcepoint for where many a life event is lived and many more are set into motion.

It is very simple to see how this pattern unfolds. Think about what you have done, throughout your life, in your pursuit of human interactions; the words you have spoken, the things you have done. Now, think about the human interactions that were forced upon your life, when some dishonest, unsavory, or unconscious person entered your existence and cause chaos either by accident and/or by their personal choice. In each of these scenarios, think about the life events that you instigated and the life events that where instigated by the other person. Whether they were good, whether they were bad, whether they helped your life, whether they destroyed your life, they were set in motion by a human being making a choice to do something/pursue something and then you were left with making the choice about how to react.

Reaction, and the choice(s) you make, in how you react, is what sets all of life in motion. Not only in your life but the life of all other people that may be affected by your choice(s)—either in your now or in the ever-expanding ripple effect of time.

As life is defined by events, how you react to them is what defines you as a human being, what defines your life, and what defines the next set of events you will encounter. It also defines the life events of all those who may encounter your reaction to your life events. Meaning, you are personally responsible for the rest of the world. Your actions equal reactions. What you do and how your handle your life events have the potential to cause a never-ending, unstoppable expansion of actions and reactions. Thus, you must be very conscious about what you do and/or do not do.

As each individual is the sourcepoint for the choices they make, each choice has the potential to spread out from that person and engulf the world. Think about how many times you have said something or done something and what you said or did caused other people to think a specific thought and/or then react in a prescribed manner. Though this may be on a very small scale, this demonstrates how what you say and do has the potential to spread outwards and define much more than any moment that any of your life events was lived within.

Each person has the potential to change the entire world. With this fact as knowledge, it is essential that you think very consciously about anything you say, anything you do, the way you react to physical and emotional thought-patterns, and the affect it may have, as that affect may come back to haunt you.

Anything you say or do, particularly anything that you say or do that directly affects another person, becomes a direct causation factor for the next events that will take place in your life. As you have directly affected another person's life, then your life becomes defined by what happens to that person because of your instigation. If it is good, then you are responsible. If it is bad, then you too are responsible. And, if you hurt anyone for any reason, what do you believe will be the consequences in the course of your life events?

Though we all wish this was not the case, not everyone is a good person. Not everyone is what they claim to be. Not everyone is honest. Not everyone is consciously trying to do good things and help people. Many, are lost in an undefined sense of self-loathing. Many are lost and defined by their psychological inadequacies. Many are simply liars, mean people, and so desire-filled and out of control of their Self that they do not care what they do to others as long as they can get their momentary fix of whatever it is they are craving. Who are you? What do you do? How do you do it? How does it affect others? And, what events does it set in motion in your life and the life of others?

People turn to the idea of god. People turn to the concept of karma. They do this to seek out a reason for why what is happening to them is happening to them. But, this is all metaphysical mumbo-jumbo. What is happening to you is defined by what you have chosen to do and what others have chosen to do with their life. What you choose to do defines, in a large part, what events you will meet in life.

You cannot define all of the events you will encounter in life because there are other people bringing their own sense of circumstance into your life. Though you cannot define all of the events you will encounter in life you can define how you react to each life event. You can rage and become angry. That is how those defined by an uncontrolled mind and unharnessed emotional reactions behave. Or, you can meet any life event with understanding.

No one ever said life is easy. We each hope to pass though life obtaining what we desire and being rewarded and content in that progress. If we live a simple, conscious life, we are more likely to not encounter large life events that have the potential to devastate us at a moments notice, brought about by those who seek to gain something from us. But, the fact is, in each of our lives, sooner-or-later, we will encounter an event that we do not like. Then, it is how consciously we encounter that moment that not only defines the next set of events we will meet in life but also how our life will be defined, because each thing that we say or do has the potential to spread forward from our self and define a much larger spectrum of reality.

Life events begin and end with you. What life events are you setting in motion?

It Is Always the Someone Else
15/Aug/2016 09:20 AM

Have ever noticed that in life everything will be going along fine and then someone comes into your realm of existence and messes everything up? I mean, this can come at you from all kinds of angles. It can be someone new in the work place or at school, someone who is rude moving in next door to you, someone sitting down next to you and being inconsiderate at a restaurant or in the movie theater, someone tormenting you on the internet, someone not paying attention and running their car into yours, on up to the larger, more calculated scale of events; it can be someone committing a crime against you, and the list goes on… The one primary element of this is that at some point, your life will be going along fine and then someone new will come into it, uninvited, and ruined everything.

This has happened to all of us. Hopefully it hasn't happened to you too much. But, once it has occurred, your life is forever altered. These invasive events can be large or they can be small but it is almost unimportant to the definition of their scale, for once it is done it is done and everything has changed.

Life is lived in moments. Each moment defines itself. Your moment can be happy or it can be sad. But, you string these moments together and that equals a lifetime—your lifetime.

For most of us, we try to be nice to people; we try to be considered and caring. We try to help and to not hurt anyone. But, not everyone is like that. There are some inconsiderate, intolerant, judgmental, and intentionally hurtful people out there. They may each have a proclaimed motivation for doing what they do and behaving in the manner they behave, but at the end of the day all that behavior does is hurt other people.

Whenever any of these invasive people enter our life we look for a way out. Whether this is accomplished by simply getting up and leaving the establishment, trying to find a new job or a better place to live, or fixing what they have broken, the quest is on. Sometimes, however, it is not that easy as this interpersonal attack may take place in a manner that is hard to defend against. Then, we are left damned by circumstance for an extended period of time.

Do the people who instigate these type of life events care? Do they say, *"Sorry?"* Probably not. They may make excuses; they may have self-defined justifications but that is as far as it will go as they are so locked into the selfishness of their own mindset that they do not even acknowledge or care about the damage they have created.

Look to your life. Think about it. Who has come into your life and truly damaged it? …Whether this damage was only in a moment or over an extended period of time, how did it feel and how did it affect your overall existence? Now, think about how did you deal with that person, that situation, and that experience? Once you have defined these factors; contemplate, through the perspective of time, how should you have dealt with it? Should you have done something differently? Or, did you take the best actions you should/could have taken in that moment? From this mental preparation and contemplation, you may be able to become more functionally aware and be able to better deal with these type of life situation and these type of people in the future.

The main thing to realize is that fist-to-fist, verbal or physical combat, is rarely the right thing to do. Sure, you may be able to win via that method but to engage this type of person only leads to further consequences instigated by their negative actions. Thus, by entering into battle with them, based upon what they have incited, may come to not only define your moment but your future, as well.

At the root/at the heart of our life is doing good things. If we want to live a good life, if we want to be remembered in a positive manner, if we want to truly make a positive contribution to the world around us, then everything we do we must initially take others into consideration. We must think about the world around us first, before we think about ourselves. This is true humility. This is true spirituality.

In life, we will each encounter people who will negatively force their way into our sphere of existence and mess up our moment. Hopefully, these forced interactions will be few and far between. Hopefully, they will not damage our life too much. But, they will occur. Understanding this, you must prepare yourself both physically and mentally to know how to react when these situations do take place. You must be more than the person who does not think of others.

People Never Think About the Effect
15/Aug/2016 09:20 AM

People never think about the effect they are having on the life of another person.

I was speaking to a shop-girl I know the other day and I asked her how she was. She tells me that both her and her boyfriend's car had been stolen in one week. *"Wow,"* I exclaimed. *"That's terrible!"*

If you think about it, that is pretty hard core. Here are two young people, attempting to make a life together, and BAM, someone enters their life, (uninvited), and really messes it up without even caring about what affect they are having on these two people.

The couple only had the basis car insurance and was not cover for theft so they were completely screwed. Screwed, here in Los Angeles, where living is expensive and they both hold low-paying jobs. Very sad.

This is the thing about life, most people never care about the effect they are having on the life of another person. They simply do what they do and think only about themselves.

Certainly, most people are not so low as to steal a car but that is not even the point. Think about it, how many bad things are done by people who do not care about the effect they are having on the life of someone else? In fact, look at yourself, how many things have you done in your life that negatively hurt someone else? Why did you do them? What was the result? Did it make you a better person? Did it make your life any better? Did the world become a better place because of what you did? Or, was someone else's life simply left hurt and damaged? And, do you even care?

How you think about others defines who you truly are.

People always look to karma and the, *"They will get theirs,"* mindset when something bad happens. And yes, probably the person who has instigated a bad action will be negatively repaid someday… But, someday is not now. And, that repayment will probably never be witnessed by the person or persons who was wronged. So what does karma actually mean?

Most people live their life from a very unconscious mindset. They only think about themselves. They only think about what they want, when they want it, and what they need. They take or they break and then they blame everyone and everything else once they get caught for their taking or their breaking.

But, life comes down to one thing, it comes down to you. What do you do? How does what you're doing help, hurt, or affect other people? If what you're doing hurts anyone, for any reason, what you are doing is wrong. It is as simple as that.

Life is not only about physical/material possesses being wrongly stolen. Life is about how you affect others and the world around you.

What do you do? What do you take? How does what you do and what you take help or hurt others? What do you think your karma will be?

A person's life is never ultimately defined by the spin they put on what they do that has hurt other people. A person's life is defined by whom they have helped. And, a small amount of hurt vastly overshadows any amount of help you may have provided.

What are doing and who are you doing it to?

Always think about other people first.

Reaching Out with Kindness
15/Aug/2016 09:20 AM

How do you encounter life? Do you meet it head-on, face-to-face with selfish thoughts, aggressive actions, and behavior demeaning to others? Or, do you smile, reach out a helping hand, and forgive instead of unleashing harsh condemnation?

How you choose to encounter life is how your life will be interpreted by others and will lead to the type of life-interactions you will have throughout your existence. And yes, how you live your life is your choice.

When you have been sad, angry, hurt, lied to, cheated, or beaten down by life who do you think about when you remember those incidences? First of all, you remember the person who brought those situations into your life. And, you most likely remember them in a negative light. Second, you remember the person who reached out a hand of helpfulness and kindness to you. That person will forever hold a place in your heart as they were the one who came to you and only expressed loving, helpful kindness.

From this simply case of life-remembrance you should easily see the best way to behave in life. But, many people do not take the time to chart their life. They do not take the time to set about on a conscious course of life-affirming action(s). Instead they are simply controlled by negative emotions instead of consciously deciding which emotions that they actually will embrace.

Do you ever ask yourself why you are doing what you are doing before you are doing it? Or, do you just do it?

Do you ever ask yourself why you are doing what you are doing before you are doing it? If you preform this conscious mental action, do you actually come up with a precise conclusion based upon a desired end-result? And, what is your desired end-result? Are you hoping to help someone or something? Are you trying to help yourself? Or, are you attempting to hurt someone or something? Or, are you just doing it to do it because you can?

Let's look at this situation for a moment… If you are trying to help yourself that can be understood to be a fairly common human desire. But, does your helping yourself hurt anyone else in the process. If you helping yourself hurts anyone, then no matter what your motivation, it cannot be seen as a conscious, good, or kind action.

If you are actually attempting to hurt anyone, for any reason at any level, who and what does that make you? What gives you the right? And, what do you think the end-results of your life is going to equal if you have unleashed this type of lower-self motivated behavior and activity onto the world?

People become empowered in various ways throughout their existence. They find a method to express themselves. Some find that they can encounter some sort of self-worth by embracing and exhibiting negative behavior. But, what is the result of negative behavior? Have you ever actually studied its patterns? Negative people think negative thoughts and continually encounter negative life experiences. It is as simple as that.

The opposite is also true, however. Think about the person who reaches out their hand to help people. They are always thought of as nice, kind, and giving. They forever meet people who want to thank them for their positive actions. And, just as we discussed in the beginning of this essay, who do you remember and how do you remember them? You remember the person that hurt you and you remember the person that helped you. One you think of negatively, the other you think of with loving positivity.

How do you want your life to be remembered? How do you want people to think about you?

My advice, do positive things, do good things, turn off your ego and help people whenever you can. Never pass judgment. Ask forgiveness for any wrongs you have committed and erase their trail of transmittal into the future.

This is your life. This life is your choice. How you live it will effect your forever and may lead to affecting the forever of other people. Thus, only say and do good things. Only help and never hurt. Only care and not judge. Mostly, be kind.

Part Two

Aphorisms

one

Life Philosophy in a Nutshell:

Say only good things. Do only good things. Help everyone you can.

Never judge anyone—their accomplishments or their creations.

Don't tell lies.

Never intentionally hurt anyone for any reason.

If you do hurt someone apologize and do all that you can to repair any damage that you've inflicted.

two

If you were going to die tomorrow what would you do today?

If you live your life embracing this mindset your everyday existence becomes far more accomplished.

three

If you think you've done nothing wrong, you are the ultimate sinner.

four

Do all of the good deeds you do today erase that one bad thing you did way back when?

five

Just because you are aware of the fact that everyday you are getting older does not mean that one day you will not wake up and realize that you are old.

six

You should really stop dreaming about the dreams that will never come true.

seven

Are you willing to change?

eight

Does your own projected negativity define your life?

Does your own projected positivity define your life?

nine

What is so wrong with your present that you have to reach back to your past to find comfort?

ten

When you've done something wrong and realize it how often do you go back and fix it?

eleven

Why do you spend your time fantasizing about things that are never going to happen?

twelve

How can you fall from grace when you have no grace?

thirteen

People don't know yet they believe that they know.

Thus, they spread fallacies as facts which creates all of the problems in this world.

fourteen

How often do you look in your rear view mirror?

fifteen

You getting revenge is only you setting yourself up for further karmic repercussions.

sixteen

If you are doing anything that hurts anyone for any reason, you will be the one who pays the price.

You cannot hurt someone without paying the consequences.

seventeen

If you don't take out the garbage your world becomes overwhelmed by garbage.

eighteen

The person who is very religious—the person who is constantly praying and talking to and about god is simply a person who does not wish to take responsibility for their own life—how what they chose to do has lead them to where they find themselves in life and what they find themselves encountering.

The concept of god and divine beings creates dependent people who do not take responsibility for themselves, their choices, and their actions.

nineteen

If you have to lie about who you are, you are no one.

twenty

If the only way you can make yourself feel good is by talking negatively about others, you are not a good person.

twenty-one

If you were to die today what would you have to show for having lived your life?

Are you satisfied with what you have accomplished?

twenty-two

When was the last time that you did something wrong that you knew was wrong but you did it anyway?

Why did you do it?

twenty-three

You are probably not going to be rewarded for helping people but if you help them then you have helped them.

twenty-four

It's easy to find a reason to pray.

twenty-five

There is a reason that there are laws.

twenty-six

You can't live another person's life for them.

twenty-seven

At any moment of your life everything can change.

twenty-eight

You can always find a reason to become angry at someone but that just tells you that you allow other people to be in control of your emotions.

twenty-nine

You can lie to yourself but you can't hide from yourself.

thirty

Who do you think about first?

The other person or yourself?

thirty-one

Who are you going to help today that you like?

Who are you going to help today that you don't like?

Do you ever wake up and question(s):

>*"Who can I help today?"*
>*"Who's life can I make better?"*

>Helping is the most holy act.

thirty-two

Unfortunately, you cannot go back in time.

thirty-three

It does not make you a better person to say and do negative things.

It does make you a better person to say and do positive things.

thirty-four

People who hate always find a new reason to hate.

People who love always find a new reason to love.

thirty-five

If you're angry at your own life and what you've experienced, you find reasons to become angry at other people.

thirty-six

How many liars have you encountered that deny they were lying when you knew that they were not telling the truth?

Liars lie then they deny.

thirty-seven

How many times a day do you lie?

Why?

thirty-eight

If you hate your life, you envy the people who don't hate their life.

If you are unhappy, you spread your unhappiness out to the world.

Bad deeds, bad words arise from what you are feeling. Instead of letting negative emotions control your life experience, what are you going to do to change your life?

thirty-nine

"I think…"

How many times have you been wrong about what you thought?

forty

How many people that you know or that know you do you hope you will never see again? That number equals a very precise definition of your life.

forty-one

What you have is what you have but what you don't have is what you want.

forty-two

Do you take the time to look at yourself to see who and what you truly are?

forty-three

If you didn't know what day of the week it was, if you didn't know the date, how would you live this day?

forty-four

God tells no one to kill.

forty-five

Do you try to fix what you've broken or do you just make excuses and deny any responsibility in the matter?

forty-six

When you say something out of frustration or anger do you ever later retract that statement in an attempt to erase any damage that it may have caused? If you don't, the negativity instigated by that statement remains out there polluting your world forever.

forty-seven

Nobody knows the pain you are feeling.

forty-eight

You can only look to the past with any sense of definition. The future is forever unknown.

forty-nine

Based on what you are doing right now, what will you have to show for it at the end of your life?

fifty

If you were to be judged in the same way as you judge others, what would people be saying about you?

fifty-one

If you were to die today what do you have to show for the life you lived?

fifty-two

Based on what you are doing right now, how will your life be remembered?

fifty-three

It is much easier to declare what is wrong with someone else than to admit what is wrong with yourself.

fifty-four

If you do bad things, you will forever be defined by the bad things you have done.

No lie you tell to yourself, no lie you tell to others will ever change the fact that what you did was bad if anything or anyone was hurt by your actions.

fifty-five

Your actions are the result of you.

    Blame no one else.

fifty-six

Do not say bad things. Do not do bad things.

There is no justification for you doing things that hurt anyone for any reason.

fifty-seven

How do you care about what you care about?

fifty-eight

What you believe to be an always may only be a sometimes.

fifty-nine

As long as you believe that you are better than someone else—as long as you believe that you are more than someone else you will forever be lost to a misdirected understanding of life because if you were actually more than someone else—if you were actually better than someone else then you would never even think or speak about them.

sixty

The longer one's life goes on unfulfilled the more bitter a person has the potential of becoming.

Fulfillment is a choice based upon a person's level of awareness.

The unfulfilled individual seeks more but more is simply a concept of something that they believe they do not have.

You can't have what you don't have.

You can only desire what you don't have but unfulfilled desire only leads to the never ending condition of lack of fulfillment.

Thus, the unfulfilled individual unfulfills themselves.

sixty-one

What is the purpose of what you are saying?

sixty-two

Who has to die so your secrets will be hidden?

sixty-three

One action—one thing that you do can change your entire life forever.

One action—one thing that you do to someone else can change their entire life forever.

Make your choices consciously.

sixty-four

Happiness is always happy.

sixty-five

When you're right you don't need to argue.

sixty-six

If someone saw the inner-workings of your mind (what you are thinking) what would they think?

sixty-seven

Right now, right here, today; what contribution are you making to the greater good of the world?

sixty-eight

You may know the truth but are you willing to tell the truth?

sixty-nine

People forever try to rationalize their deeds and their actions.

Do you ever simply say, *"I was wrong?"*

seventy

You can't make somebody care.

seventy-one

When someone tells you a lie and you believe it to be the truth what does that make it?

seventy-two

What do you do when you don't want to face the truth?

seventy-three

If you don't think about your actions, if you don't care about the repercussion they will unleash, why should anyone care about you?

seventy-four

I'm not asking you to agree with me, I'm just asking you to think.

seventy-five

Do rude people ever care that they are rude?

Do unthinking people ever care that they are unthinking?

Do selfish people ever care that they are selfish?

Do liars ever care that they are telling a lie?

seventy-six

Have you ever gone out of your way to do something nice for a person you do not like?

seventy-seven

Do you ever admit the fault is yours?

seventy-eight

Who gave you the right to judge?

seventy-nine

How do you say you're sorry?

eighty

If you are thinking about someone else, you are thinking about the wrong person.

If you are talking about someone else, you are talking about the wrong person.

All life begins and ends with you. Thus, all good and bad emulates from you.

There is one person you should be focusing on and refining. That person is you.

eighty-one

When you've done something bad or said something bad that affected another person, do you think that action will not to come back to haunt you even if you weren't seen doing it?

eighty-two

Saying something that isn't true never makes it the truth. It only makes the world know that you are a lair.

eighty-three

The person who insults other people is simply trying to take the focus off what is lacking in their own life.

The successful person has no need to insult anyone.

eighty-four

How many lies do you have to tell to make yourself appear to be something worthwhile?

The amount of lies you tell defies who you truly are.

eighty-five

Just because you believe something to be true does not make it true.

eighty-six

Who have you hurt?

Why have you hurt them?

What would you be willing to go through to wiped your karma clean?

eighty-seven

Everyone wants the other person to be paid back for their bad actions but no one wants to be paid back for their bad deeds.

eighty-eight

Empowerment based upon the critique of others only provides the life of the critiqued with more value and the life of the critiquer with less.

eighty-nine

How much do you ever truly know about another person?

ninety

You can't ask a person what's wrong with them when they are too lost to understand that something is actually wrong with them.

ninety-one

It is only the low-minded individual who takes pride in the damage that they create.

ninety-two

If you find something that brings you peace that is your ticket to the higher mind.

ninety-three

Never is Never.

ninety-four

Self-involved is the ultimate definition of the person who does not have the ability to truly care about other people.

ninety-five

Can you be yourself in all life-circumstances and with all the people who define your life? If you can, you are who you are. If you can't you need to come to new conclusions either about your definition of you or the world's definition of you.

ninety-six

If you look outside yourself to find yourself, your-self will forever be something that you are not.

ninety-seven

The seek cannot find. The seeker can only seek.

ninety-eight

More is more only when it equals something more.

More is less when all, *"The More,"* does is burden your life.

ninety-nine

"I get it."

When you finally get it, you've got it. You understand.

How much of your life have you spend doing and pursing when you did not understand the rules of the game?

one-hundred

Does your doing equal what you want your doing to equal?

one-hundred-one

If you are outside listening to the words of other people your world will be defined by what you hear.

one-hundred-two

Can you be whole based upon a life that is defined by a lie?

one-hundred-three

When people look at you what do you see?

When you look at yourself what do you see?

Is what you see the same as what other people see?

one-hundred-four

As creation is understood to be the ultimate purpose of life, what are you creating?

one-hundred-five

If you disguise who you are for any reason ten who are you?

one-hundred-six

Can you be yourself when you're not being yourself?

one-hundred-seven

We all want to be free.

Are you willing to pay the price to be free?

one-hundred-eight

Life is easy if you understand how to let life me easy.

The secret?

I can't tell you. You have to find it out for yourself.

THE ZEN

www.ingramcontent.com/pod-product-compliance
Lightning Source LLC
Chambersburg PA
CBHW070736170426
43200CB00007B/546